S0-AYF-679

CONTENTS

97 0901

GEN. (RET.) WERNER VON SCHEVEN (R) IS INTERVIEWED FOR "THE GERMANS." EXECUTIVE PRODUCER ANDREW WALWORTH (L); EXECUTIVE EDITOR JEFFREY GEDMIN (M).

JEFFREY GEDMIN (R), TAKING A BREAK FROM A SHOOT WITH CAMERAMAN BRUCE KISSAL (L) AND SOUNDMAN SVEN (M).

ALICE KELLY (R), CO-PRODUCER FOR "THE GERMANS," WORKS WITH A TEAM IN BERLIN.

THE GERMANS

PORTRAIT OF A NEW NATION

TODAY, FIVE YEARS AFTER UNIFICATION, GERMANY IS EMERGING AS EUROPE'S MOST INFLUENTIAL COUNTRY. ITS SIZE, GEOGRAPHIC LOCATION, ECONOMIC STRENGTH, AND MILITARY POTENTIAL ASSURE GERMANY AN IMPORTANT ROLE IN SHAPING DEVELOPMENTS IN THE POST-COLD WAR ERA. WHO ARE THE GERMANS TODAY?

"THE GERMANS: PORTRAIT OF A NEW NATION" IS A ONE-HOUR TELEVISION DOCUMENTARY THAT PROFILES GERMANY AND ITS PEOPLE FIVE YEARS AFTER UNIFICATION. THE PROGRAM IS PRODUCED BY NEW RIVER MEDIA, INC. OF WASHINGTON, D.C. THIS COMPANION BOOK PRESENTS INTERVIEWS WITH THE EXTRAORDINARY INDIVIDUALS, BOTH PRIVATE CITIZENS AND LEADING EXPERTS, WHOM WE WERE PRIVILEGED TO MEET.

ACKNOWLEDGMENTS

Thanks goes to the American Enterprise Institute and AEI's president, Christopher C. DeMuth, and executive vice president, David Gerson. A special thanks also goes to Dan Fata, Marta Ferrer, Rachel Lebenson, Christopher Hayes, and Alison Boyd. A special debt of gratitude is owed to Stacey Thomas. Generous support for the television documentary was provided by the Arcana Foundation, BMW AG, the RIAS Berlin Commission, General Motors/Europe, Nordstern Colonia Insurance, Lufthansa German Airlines, Kempinski Hotels, and Hilton Hotels. The support of the German Information Center in New York was instrumental for the publication of this book.

EDITORIAL NOTE

The following collection of texts is based on transcripts from videotaped interviews for the TV documentary "The Germans: Portrait of a New Nation." All interviews were conducted between January and June 1995.

Despite the rich academic literature on German unification and its consequences, the American public does not have easy access to authentic voices of Germans whose lives have been affected by the events of 1989 and 1990.

This companion book makes fuller portions of the interviews available to interested readers. We also hope that some readers might find this book helpful as a teaching tool.

The interviews have been shortened and undergone slight stylistic changes.

MATTHIAS E. LEITNER
Associate Editor

EXECUTIVE PRODUCER ANDREW WALWORTH RELAXES
WITH ONE OF THE LÖBNER CHILDREN DURING A BREAK.

MATTHIAS E. LEITNER, ASSOCIATE EDITOR AND
PRODUCTION ASSISTANT.

BERLIN CAMERAMAN SEBASTIAN PREPARES A SHOT.

GERMANY FACT SHEET

(A Brief History Since 1945)

1945
World War Two Ends. Germany surrenders unconditionally, marking the end of the war in Europe. The Allies divide Germany into four occupation zones.

1948
Berlin Blockade. Western powers provide aid to the Soviet blockaded city of Berlin.

1954
West Germany Joins NATO. The Federal Republic of Germany is allowed to join in the common defense of the North Atlantic Community.

1958
European Community Comes Into Operation. The Federal Republic of Germany is one of the original six member countries.

1961
Berlin Wall Goes Up. East Germany seals the border between East and West Berlin by building the Berlin Wall. Its purpose is to deter mass exodus of East Germans into West Germany.

1973
United Nations Extends Membership. Both West and East Germany are granted membership rights.

1989
Berlin Wall Comes Down. The embodiment

of a failed system comes crashing down and
with it the East German state, setting the stage
for German unification.

1990
Germany Unites as One Nation. After nearly
40 years of living as a divided people, East and
West Germans are unified under one flag and
one democratic government.

1991
Maastricht Treaty Signed. Twelve European
Community nations, including Germany,
agree to create the European Union.
Berlin Named Capital of United Germany.
The Bundestag votes to make Berlin the new
national capital.

1992
**Outbreaks of Extreme Right Wing Violence
Hit Germany.** Many cities throughout
Germany report attacks on foreigners as well
as a rise in xenophobic attitudes.

1993
**Germany Uses Troops For First Time in
Out-of-Area Operations.** The German government sends 1,700 German soldiers to participate in the UN mission in Somalia.

1994
Russian Troops Leave German Soil. German
unification is completed as Russia withdraws
its soldiers from the former East Germany.
Kohl Reelected. In power since 1982, Helmut
Kohl is reelected German chancellor and prepares to eclipse Konrad Adenauer's historic
fourteen year tenure in office.

THE FAMILIES

After a four year wait, the Wilfarts were allowed
to leave East Germany in 1987. Today they live
in Heiningen, a small town near Stuttgart in the
western state of Baden-Württemberg.

The Löbners live in Ilmenau, a city of 30,000 inhabitants, in the eastern state of Thuringia. Christel works in neighboring Erfurt as an accountant for the *Deutsche Bahn*, the new all-German railway. Christel's husband George is a music teacher at a secondary school in Ilmenau. The couple has two young daughters, ages five and six.

BIRGIT DE LONG

Birgit De Long lives in Frankfurt am Main
and works in the music industry. She is a sales
representative for mms-Eurodistribution, a
company based in Frankfurt with offices in
New York and Amsterdam.

WERNER PETERS

Werner Peters is a writer and community organizer living in Cologne. He owns the Hotel Chelsea, its adjoining restaurant and cafe, as well as a new upscale restaurant in downtown Cologne. His son Guido works for British Telecom in Germany.

THE COMMENTATORS

CHRISTOPH BERTRAM
Diplomatic Correspondent, *Die Zeit*

DANIEL COHN-BENDIT
Official, Frankfurt City Government

DAVID HERMAN
Chairman, Adam Opel AG

WERNER HOLZER
Editor-in-Chief (ret.), *Frankfurter Rundschau*

FRANZ KADELL
Acting Editor-in-Chief, *Magdeburger Volksstimme*

BURKHARD KOCH
Fachhochschule Potsdam

ROBERT M. KIMMITT
U.S. Ambassador to Germany, 1991-1993

OTTO GRAF LAMBSDORFF
Former Chairman, Free Democratic Party

COL. BERND MÜLLER
Commander, Rapid Reaction Force, Oldenburg

JULIUS SCHOEPS
Potsdam University

ANGELA STENT
Georgetown University

GEN. (RET.) WERNER VON SCHEVEN
Former Commander-in-Chief Corps and Territorial Command East

NORBERT WALTER
Senior Economist, Deutsche Bank

GEN. (RET.) WERNER VON SCHEVEN

BURKHARD KOCH

DAVID HERMAN

PART ONE

NOVEMBER 1989

THE FALL OF THE BERLIN WALL MARKED A
NEW ERA FOR GERMANY AND THE WORLD. FOR
MANY GERMANS, A LONG-HELD DREAM HAD
BECOME REALITY: AFTER 40 YEARS OF DIVI-
SION, GERMANY WAS ONE COUNTRY AGAIN.

TOP LEFT: THE BERLIN WALL AT BRANDENBURG GATE,
NOVEMBER 1989.

BOTTOM LEFT: "ATTENTION: YOU ARE LEAVING WEST
BERLIN." EAST GERMAN AUTHORITIES ERECTED THE
BERLIN WALL IN 1961 TO STOP THE ESCAPE OF ITS CITI-
ZENS TO THE WEST.

PHOTO COURTESY OF GERMAN INFORMATION CENTER, NEW YORK.

INTERVIEWER: Georg, wo warst Du am 9. November 1989, und wie hast Du eigentlich vom Fall der Mauer erfahren?

GEORG: Am 9. November 1989 habe ich laufend die Nachrichten verfolgt und irgendwie war es für mich—unwahrscheinlich, daß nun die Berliner Bevölkerung dort ohne weitere Komplikationen und Formalitäten auf die andere Seite gehen konnte. Daß ich also ohne Probleme dort hätte hinfahren können, und rübergehen, um dort meine Verwandten, die ich in West-Berlin habe, zu besuchen. Als ich am nächsten Morgen in die Schule kam, war das logischerweise das erste Thema. Da kam auch schon ein Kollege und sagte: Eben hab' ich einen Anruf bekommen von drüben. Der dicke Meier, der ist schon nach drüben gefahren und hat das ausgenutzt. Ich weiß noch was es für ein erhebendes und kaum zu beschreibendes, sagenhaftes Gefühl war, als ich mit meiner Frau und den beiden Kindern das erste Mal nach Coburg fuhr. Das ist schon so sehr Vergangenheit und Selbstverständlichkeit geworden, obwohl man es eigentlich gar nicht vergessen sollte.

INTERVIEWER: Was für ein Gefühl hast Du da gehabt?

CHRISTEL: Es war irgendwie ein ganz tolles Gefühl zu sehen, daß die Grenze durchlässig ist. Auf der anderen Seite dachte ich wieder: Das kann nicht sein, ist die Grenze jetzt wirklich auf? Ich bin ja nun erst 1964 geboren, in tiefster DDR-Zeit praktisch aufgewachsen, vom System und meiner ganzen Bildung her so erzogen, daß es da halt eine Mauer gibt, eine Mauer, die undurchdringlich ist. Es wurde immer gesagt, die Grenze bleibt ewig bestehen.

INTERVIEWER: George, where were you on November 9, 1989, and how did you receive news of the fall of the Wall?

GEORGE: On November 9, 1989, I was continuously following the news, and somehow it was—how should I say—unbelievable. I had seen the Berlin Wall myself, and it seemed unbelievable that Berliners could now cross the border without any complications and formalities. It was unbelievable that I could now travel to West Berlin and see my relatives. And as I walked into school the next morning, everybody was buzzing with the news of our friend Meier. A colleague of mine approached me immediately and said, "I just had a phone call from 'over there' from Meier, who already drove across." I still remember what an elated and almost indescribable feeling it was when my wife, the two children, and I drove to Coburg for the first time. That was one of the most beautiful moments in my life. I will never forget it.

INTERVIEWER: What kind of feelings did you have then?

CHRISTEL: It was a wonderful feeling to see that the border was open, but on the other hand I thought, "This can't be. Is the border really open?" I was born in 1964, in the harshest of East German times; I was raised within this system, within this whole educational system. Growing up, it was so self-evident, that there was the Wall, a border which was impenetrable. It was always said that the border would stand forever. As solid and permanent as the frontier between both parts of Germany

Ich hatte mir zwar gewünscht, den anderen Teil Deutschlands kennenzulernen, aber innerlich habe ich nie geglaubt, jemals zu erleben, daß die Grenze durchlässig wird, daß ich den anderen Teil Deutschlands sehen kann und die Leute, die die gleiche Sprache sprechen wie ich, jemals besuchen kann. Ich konnte das einfach nicht fassen, daß jetzt etwas passiert war, von dem ich wirklich nur geträumt hatte. Gleich nach der Wende wurden Buslinien eingerichtet, zum Beispiel von Ilmenau nach Coburg oder nach Neustadt in der Nähe von Coburg, da der Besucherandrang erst mal von uns aus nach Bayern ging wegen der Grenznähe. Weder die damalige Deutsche Reichsbahn vermochte, die Leute zu transportieren, die auf die andere Seite der deutschen Grenze wollten, noch war es mit dem Individualverkehr möglich, den Besucherstrom in irgendeiner Art und Weise zu bewältigen. Es wurde sehr flexibel reagiert von den wenigen privaten Busunternehmen, die bestanden, als auch vom Kraftverkehr, wie er damals hieß. Beide beschlossen spontan: Wir machen eine Buslinie. Es gab Karten im Vorverkauf, die Leute standen nach den Karten an, und es war unheimlich, das zu erleben. Jeder dachte: Ich muß jetzt ganz schnell rüberfahren. Auch ich dachte: Du mußt jetzt ganz schnell versuchen, wenigstens einmal auf die andere Seite von Deutschland zu kommen, denn es könnte morgen schon wieder anders sein. Heute ist die Grenze auf, heute können wir fahren. So kannst Du wenigstens sagen, Du warst mal drüben, und hast das gesehen. Es war ein ganz unbeschreibliches Gefühl, als der Bus sich dann dem Grenzbereich näherte; dort waren so kleine Häuschen aufgestellt, bevor man überhaupt in den grenznahen Bereich hineinfuhr. Mir selbst

seemed to be, I could never believe it would disappear some day.

I wanted to get to know the other part of Germany, but inside I never believed that I would experience the opening of the border, that I could see the other part of Germany, and that I could visit the people who speak the same language as I do. I could not grasp that something had occurred, of which I had only *dreamed.* Right after the fall of the Wall, a bus line was established, for example, from Ilmenau to Coburg and to Neustadt near Coburg, because the wave of visitors from here to Bavaria was so huge, neither the German Reichsbahn [East German railway], nor private transit could accommodate the wave of visitors to the other side of the border. The bus companies reacted very flexibly, both the few private companies that existed, as well as public transport. Both decided simultaneously to

war das gänzlich unbekannt, da ich ja nie irgendwie in den Sicherheitsbereich hineingekommen
war oder auch nur in die Nähe. Dann kam der
ehemalige Grenzübergang mit einem
Wärterhäuschen. Die Grenzposten standen noch
bei unserem ersten Besuch und der große
Balken, der dann im Bedarfsfall herausgefahren
werden konnte, um unerwünschte Ausreisen zu
verhindern, der stand noch da. Es war unheimlich überwältigend, im Bus zu sitzen und das
Gefühl zu haben: Du weißt, Du fährst jetzt nach
Bayern. Das Schild stand vor uns, ein großes
rundes, ich weiß es noch, mit der Aufschrift
"Bayern grüßt seine Gäste". Es war unvorstellbar,
daß man jetzt wirklich reisen konnte. Die
Grenzbeamten kamen rein, sahen sich unsere
Ausweise an und wünschten gute Fahrt. Wir hat-

establish a bus line. Tickets could be purchased beforehand; the people stood in line for the tickets. It was strange to experience. Everyone thought, even I myself thought, "I must get over quickly, to try and make it at least once to the other side of Germany, because the situation could change tomorrow. Today the border is open, today we can go. So at the least you can say, you were over there, you saw it." It was an indescribable feeling when the bus neared the border; there were little guard houses before one even came closer to the border. This was all completely new to me, since I had never been to the border area or even near it. Then came the former main checkpoint with the big guard post. The border posts were still there at the

EAST MEETS WEST AFTER THE FALL OF THE BERLIN WALL IN NOVEMBER 1989.

ten bei unserer ersten Fahrt die Kinder dabei. Sie bekamen einen Kaugummi und eine Apfelsine geschenkt. Jana als Baby mit zwei Monaten konnte ja damit nichts anfangen, aber schon allein die Geste war etwas wert. Selbst im Bus hatte ich immer noch Angst: Wenn jetzt die Grenzbeamten reinkommen, lassen sie Dich nicht fahren; die werfen Dich jetzt wieder aus dem Bus, und es war für mich eine unheimliche Genugtuung, als sie wieder ausstiegen und uns allen im Bus gute Fahrt wünschten, als sich der Bus in Bewegung setzte und das Schild "Bayern grüßt seine Gäste" hinter sich zurückließ. Ich wußte, ich bin jetzt drüben und mir kamen die Tränen. Auch heute noch, wenn wir die gleiche Straße befahren, muß ich daran denken. Die Grenzanlagen von früher sind zwar beseitigt, aber ich glaube, ich werde das nie vergessen, weil für mich eigentlich das eingetreten ist, was unvorstellbar war. Ein absoluter Wunschtraum hat sich jetzt erfüllt. ■

WERNER PETERS

time of our first visit, and the big beam, which could be used to prevent unauthorized cross-border traffic was there as well. It was overwhelming to sit in the bus and have the feeling that you are driving to Bavaria! The sign stood before us, a big round one, I still remember it, with the words, "Bavaria greets its guests." It was inconceivable that one could now really drive across, and the border guards came in, checked our identification papers, and wished us all a safe trip. On our first trip, we had our children with us. They got a piece of chewing gum and an orange as a present. Jana being only a baby of two months could not do much with her present, but the gesture alone was something. Inside the bus, I was still afraid that, when the border guards stepped up, they would throw us out of the bus. It was amazing to me when they got off the bus again and wished us a safe trip, and the bus began to move, leaving the sign "Bavaria greets its guests" behind. Then I knew that I was definitely on the other side of the border, and I started to cry. Even today, when we drive on the same road—the border installations have been removed—I will never forget that moment, because for me the unimaginable became a reality. An absolute dream had now become reality.

WERNER PETERS

INTERVIEWER: If you think about November 9th, 1989, this great event, can you remember where you were, how you heard the news? What did you think?

WERNER: It was on November 9th when

the Berlin Wall came down, or rather when it was opened. Yes, I had a fantastic experience actually. I was in the United States during the fall—I started to travel there more regularly in the fall of 1989, and I moved back and forth to Germany frequently for business. And there was something building up. I heard it on the news, and I read it in the papers. Yet nobody ever expected anything to happen. By chance, I boarded a plane to Germany on the evening of November 9th, and when I arrived in Frankfurt I saw this huge headline in the *Bildzeitung* daily, "The Wall has Come Down." I had tears in my eyes. It was incredible.

INTERVIEWER: What did you do then?

WERNER: Well, I can't remember. I said I was almost crying. And, you know, people were running around. We were talking to each other saying, "Isn't this incredible?" Since we all had just arrived on this flight, during the 9th, and we hadn't seen anything, we were all surprised. So we talked to each other. It was a funny thing. You know, we were just so happy, incredibly happy. I think when I arrived here in Cologne, nobody was talking about anything else. And then, of course, we were glued to the TV screen, and we saw pictures of people walking through the border checkpoints. And I think it was on that day when the gates at the borders were opened, and people were driving through with their Trabants, you know, their little East German cars. We were greeting them here in West Germany, and people from West Germany went over there. It was a huge celebration and a fantastic experience, even for us who were only able to watch it on TV. ■

PART TWO

EAST GERMAN LEGACIES

EAST GERMANS HAVE EXPERIENCED REMARKABLE—AND SOMETIMES PAINFUL—ECONOMIC AND SOCIAL CHANGES. THEY ALSO FACE TROUBLING QUESTIONS ABOUT THE PAST.

FIVE YEARS AFTER UNIFICATION, IT HAD BECOME CLEAR TO MOST GERMANS THAT THEIR COUNTRY WOULD NOT RECOVER FROM 40 YEARS OF COMMUNIST RULE IN THE EAST AS QUICKLY AS THEY HAD IMAGINED.

STATUE OF LENIN STILL STANDING IN SCHWERIN IN MAY 1995.

PHOTO COURTESY OF MARIA WILLIAMS

INTERVIEWER: Die Wende. Was bedeutet das für Euch?

STEFAN: Was bedeutet es für mich? Im Prinzip nicht viel Positives, denn wir waren ja schon in Westdeutschland beziehungsweise in der Bundesrepublik. Für uns persönlich war das Positivste an der Wende, daß wir wieder einmal nach Ostdeutschland zurückfahren konnten, um unsere Mütter zu besuchen. Denn man hatte uns ja damals gesagt: Wenn Ihr einmal aus der DDR weggeht, dann werdet Ihr nie wieder zurückkommen können oder Eure Familie sehen dürfen. Politisch gesehen...ja, die Wende, was hat sie jetzt gebracht? Im Nachhinein muß ich sagen, ich bin schwer enttäuscht von der Wende, obwohl ich mich über die Wiedervereinigung gefreut habe. Ich freue mich nach wie vor über die Wiedervereinigung, aber so wie sie gelaufen ist, ist das völlig inakzeptabel. Ich kann gar nicht nachvollziehen, was da passiert ist, beziehungsweise nicht passiert ist. Zum Beispiel die juristische, strafrechtliche Aufarbeitung in Ostdeutschland ist praktisch Null, nichts ist passiert. Außer vielleicht, daß der Herr Mielke, der ehemalige Stasi-Chef dieses *Bonzenregimes*, als einziger im Gefängnis sitzt, und zwar für einen Mord, den er 1932 an zwei Polizisten begangen hat. Also, da krieg' ich Zustände, wenn ich daran denke, daß er nicht einmal für die Maueropfer oder ähnliches bestraft wird, sondern für einen Mord, der—wie lange ist das jetzt her—über sechzig Jahre her ist. Und diese ganzen anderen Verbrecher aus dem Politbüro und der Regierung? Jeder kennt den Fall Honecker, und Krenz läuft noch frei herum und so weiter. Das ist für mich dermaßen ent-

INTERVIEWER: The fall of the Wall and unification, what does it mean to you?

STEFAN: Basically, not a lot of positive things, since we were already in the West; that is, in West Germany. For us personally, the best thing (there were surely other positive things, personally speaking) was that we were able to go back to East Germany again to see our mothers. Because before we had been told: "If you leave East Germany, there will be no more coming back for you or visits to the family." Politically speaking...well, what has unification brought us? Looking back, I have to say I'm very disappointed. I am still happy about reunification, but the way it took place is completely unacceptable. The legal accountability in East Germany is practically zero; nothing has happened. Except that Mr. Mielke, the former Stasi secret police chief of this criminal regime, went to jail; for a murder he committed in 1932. Well, it drives me crazy if I consider that he is not being punished for the people who were killed at the Wall, but for a murder that happened more than sixty years ago. And what about all these other criminals in East Germany? Everybody is familiar with the Honecker case, and Krenz is still free. I am so disappointed by this. I lived under this regime.

INTERVIEWER: What about the issue of collaboration?

STEFAN: In my opinion, the little people were the worst. Today, I believe that these collaborators, these denouncers and informers—there were thousands and hundreds of thousands—they were the ones who provided the

> **DAS SIND MEINES ERACHTENS DIE SCHLIMMSTEN...DIE MITLÄUFER.**

täuschend, weil man ja unter diesem Regime gelebt hat.

INTERVIEWER: Was bedeutet für Dich der Begriff "Mitläufertum"?

STEFAN: Das sind meines Erachtens die Schlimmsten. Man lernt ja immer dazu, und ich bin heute der Meinung, daß diese Mitläufer, diese Intriganten und Denunzianten, die es ja tausend-, hunderttausendfach gab—was weiß ich, wie oft—daß nur die das Regime aufrechterhalten konnten. Wie man das vielleicht schon einmal von 1933 bis 1945 in Deutschland hatte, nicht wahr? Wie bei uns zum Beispiel im Haus. Nachdem wir den Ausreiseantrag eingereicht hatten, wurden wir ja sofort unter Beobachtung gestellt, und da fühlte sich ein älteres Ehepaar berufen, jeden Besucher, der in unserer Wohnung ein-und ausging (Westbesuch war ganz schlimm, wenn man irgendwann einmal Besuch bekam aus der Bundesrepublik), mit minutiösen Eintragungen zu kontrollieren: Wann sind die Leute gekommen, wann haben die das Haus verlassen, was haben sie mitgebracht an Geschenken, vielleicht ein Paket oder vielleicht eine Schallplatte oder so.

BRIGITTE: Obwohl man eben auch sagen muß, daß es viele gab, die das um des eigenen Vorteils willen gemacht haben. Die haben zu Hause eigentlich ganz anders gedacht, aber das für ihr berufliches Fortkommen getan, weil sie sonst eben diese oder jene Stellung nicht bekommen hätten. Also, von denen gab es sehr viele.

regime its stability, just like in Germany, from 1933 to 1945. In our building, for instance, after we had filed the application papers to emigrate, we were immediately placed under surveillance, and an elderly couple felt the need to keep a meticulous record of every single visitor who came and went (visitors from the West were a particularly bad thing): "When did these people arrive, when did they leave the building, and what did they bring as presents; a package maybe or a record or other things?"

BRIGITTE: One also has to say that there were many who did this simply for the sake of their own advancement. They had a different attitude at home, but they did these things in order to advance their careers, as they would not have gotten this or that job otherwise. There were a lot of these people.

INTERVIEWER: Are you at all interested today in seeing your own Stasi file?

STEFAN: Yes, but we have been trying for years without any result. Just a few weeks ago, I called Erfurt regarding this matter, where the head office for the southern districts of former East Germany is located. My file is not there. It is simply gone.

BRIGITTE: We even hired a lawyer to look into this.

STEFAN: That's right, a lawyer who lives here in the building. You always think that this kind of help would speed things up.

BRIGITTE: Yet the file cannot be found any more.

INTERVIEWER: Habt Ihr denn heute eigentlich selbst Interesse daran, in Eure Stasi-Akte reinzuschauen?

STEFAN: Doch, aber man bemüht sich seit Jahren, und es läuft nichts. Ich hab erst vor einigen Wochen in Erfurt angerufen. Dort ist die Zentrale für die Südbezirke der ehemaligen DDR; meine Akte ist angeblich gar nicht da.

BRIGITTE: Wir haben das sogar über einen Anwalt laufen lassen.

STEFAN: Ja richtig, über einen Rechtsanwalt, der hier im Haus wohnt. Man glaubt immer, daß so etwas vielleicht schneller geht.

BRIGITTE: Aber die Akte ist nicht mehr aufzufinden.

STEFAN: Die letzte Antwort, die ich bekommen habe, telefonisch vor einigen Wochen, war folgende (wobei wir schon länger wußten, daß die Akte angeblich nicht da ist): Ich soll im Erfurter Stadtarchiv nachschauen. Also, für mich ist das unklar; im Erfurter Stadtarchiv, da sind vielleicht Dinge von Martin Luther, nicht wahr? Also, ich bin nicht Martin Luther und schon gar nicht so wichtig. Für mich war das geradezu unfaßbar, um das nochmal zu sagen, unfaßbar. Mit Sicherheit will man auch gar nicht die Aufklärung der Stasi-Akten, und der Herr Bundeskanzler Kohl hat ja auch mal vor geraumer Zeit gesagt: Er wüßte, wenn er in der Richtung das Sagen hätte, was mit diesen Akten geschehen würde. Das ist für mich eindeutig: er will sie schließen. So hat er's nicht gesagt, er hat nur gesagt, er wüßte was er machen würde, wenn er das alleinige Sagen hätte über diese Akten. Und das kann ja nicht bedeuten, sie offenzuhalten, denn offen sind sie ja noch, sondern das bedeutet Schließung, um endlich den Mantel des Schweigens über die Vergangenheit

STEFAN: The last response I had on the telephone was the following (although we had known for a long time that the file had allegedly vanished): I should look in the Erfurt city archives. Well, this makes no sense to me. In the Erfurt city archive, you would perhaps find things by Martin Luther. Well, I am not Martin Luther and by no means as important. To me, this was almost unbelievable. Let me repeat this, *unbelievable.* Certainly they are not really willing to investigate the Stasi files, and Chancellor Kohl has also said that he would know what to do with these files if he were in charge of them. It is clear to me, he wants them closed; he wants to close them. He did not put it that way. He only said that he would know what to do if he were in charge of these files. And that cannot mean keeping them open, after all, since they are still accessible. It means closing them in order to finally pull the curtain on the past. They want to put this

zu breiten. Man soll eben zur Gegenwart übergehen: "Friede, Freude, Eierkuchen", gehen wir zur Tagesordnung über.

BRIGITTE: So kann man eigentlich nur reden, wenn man damit nichts zu tun hatte. Aber diese vielen Betroffenen, die können das nicht so einfach vergessen und sagen: So, jetzt ist es halt abgetan damit. Das geht nicht, wenn man selbst betroffen war, und viele sind ja viel, viel schlimmer betroffen gewesen als wir. Die saßen ewig im Gefängnis oder im Zuchthaus. Das ist schon schlimm.

CHRISTEL AND GEORGE LÖBNER

INTERVIEWER: Was gibt es heute in Ilmenau im Vergleich zu damals?

GEORGE: Na, heute im Vergleich zu damals kann man vor allem Dinge auf elektrotechnischem Gebiet oder elektronischem Gebiet anführen. Wenn wir einfache Taschenrechner nehmen, die waren astronomisch teuer. Ein Taschenrechner, den wir heute für zehn, zwölf Mark kaufen, hätte zu DDR-Zeiten vielleicht 250-300 oder noch mehr Mark gekostet. Das ist nicht irgendwie aus der Luft gegriffen, das ist Tatsache. Und es war in Schulen nicht in der Form verbreitet, Taschenrechner einzusetzen, was dann höchstens an den Universitäten der Fall war, wo man sich's dann leisten mußte.

INTERVIEWER: Und bei Euch persönlich, wie stand es mit Auto und Telefon?

GEORGE: Ja, ich hatte 1978 ein Telefon beantragt, und da hat man mich gefragt: Was haben Sie für wichtige Funktionen? Ich sagte: Ich bin Lehrer und sonstiges. Ich war weder in

matter to rest and do business as usual, to live happily ever after.

BRIGITTE: You can talk like this only if you were not affected. The many victims, however, cannot simply forget about it and say, "Well, that was then." And many people were rotting in prison, so much worse off than we ever were. It's really terrible.

CHRISTEL AND GEORGE LÖBNER

INTERVIEWER: What is available today in contrast to East German times?

GEORGE: Well, compared to former times, you can above all cite things in the electronics sector. Or, if you take simple pocket calculators, their prices were sky-high. A pocket calculator that we can buy for ten, twelve Marks ($8) today, would have cost perhaps 250 to 300 Marks ($175 to $210) or more during East German times. This is a fact. And in schools the use of pocket calculators was not so widespread, only at the university level, where you had to be able to afford one.

INTERVIEWER: What about you personally, your car or telephone?

GEORGE: Well, I had applied for a telephone in 1978 and they asked me, "What important tasks do you perform?" I said I was a teacher and so forth. I was neither a party member nor with the secret police. I wasn't a super-important functionary either, so they put me on the waiting list, and I did not get a telephone until 1992. I had to wait fourteen years for my telephone. Your own car, that was something utopian for us back then.

CHRISTEL: The wait for a car was ten, twelve

der Partei noch in der Staatssicherheit. Dann war ich auch kein hochwichtiger sonstiger Funktionär, also mußte ich erst mal auf die Warteliste und habe zu DDR-Zeiten kein Telefon mehr bekommen, sondern erst 1992. Ich habe also 14 Jahre auf mein Telefon warten müssen. Ein eigenes Auto, das war Utopie für uns damals. Wenn es nach den Anmeldefristen gegangen wäre, hätten wir es heute noch nicht.

CHRISTEL: Die Wartezeit für ein Auto betrug damals etwa zehn, zwölf Jahre, und es gab bei uns im wesentlichen ja nur zwei Autotypen, die in der damaligen DDR hergestellt wurden: Das waren der Trabant und der Wartburg. Die wurden auch meist nach ein-und demselben Schema gebaut, obgleich mehrere Projekteure in den Autohäusern andere Prototypen entwickelt hatten. Aber es war halt nicht beabsichtigt, daß sich das äußere Aussehen der Autos verändern sollte. Man wollte eben alles beim Gleichen belassen. Aber um noch einmal drauf zurückzukommen, auf den Einzug der Technik: Der Einzug der modernen Technik ist auch ein Grund dafür, weswegen soviele Leute entlassen werden oder ihre Tätigkeit wechseln müssen. Früher beispielsweise waren in einem Stellwerk mindestens fünf oder zehn Mann beschäftigt. Heute kann das einer allein; er braucht nur aufs Knöpfchen zu drücken, während früher einer eben rausgehen und vieles manuell regeln mußte.

INTERVIEWER: George, wie ist die

years back then, and there were basically only two types of cars produced in the former East Germany. They were built according to the same design, although engineers in several car plants had developed different prototypes. Yet it was not intended, after all, that the outer appearance of cars should change. They simply wanted to keep things as they were. But coming back to the advent of new technology: The advent of new technology is also a reason why so many people have lost or had to change jobs. Formerly, for instance, a railway switching station employed at least five to ten persons. Today, one alone can do the job. He only has to press a button, whereas formerly you had to go outside and regulate many things by hand.

INTERVIEWER: George, what is the atmosphere in school like, compared to before?

GEORGE: Previously students were very

CHILDREN PLAY ON AN EAST GERMAN TRABANT
CONVERTED TO PLAYGROUND EQUIPMENT
AT AN EAST BERLIN SCHOOL.

Stimmung in der Schule im Vergleich zu DDR-Zeiten damals?

GEORGE: In den alten Zeiten—also sagen wir mal zu Zeiten der DDR über 40 Jahre hinweg—war die Einbindung der Schüler in die Pionierorganisation, die Freie deutsche Jugend, die FdJ, sehr straff. Man war von staatlicher Seite her sehr interessiert daran, daß die Kinder und Jugendlichen dort organisiert waren, damit man sie einen Teils ideologisch auf den sogenannten richtigen Weg bringen konnte. Denn wenn man die SED betrachtet, so war die FdJ deren Parteischmiede, wo man einmal später Nachwuchskader für die SED werben konnte. Ähnlich war es ja auch in der Pionierorganisation: Da gab es nämlich schon bestimmte Leute, die schon dort ganz stark als Kader dieser Organisation eingebunden wurden. Dort wurde im Rahmen dieser Organisation viel organisiert bis hin zum Lernen—was manchmal auch nicht schlecht war, besonders wenn man gemeinsame Veranstaltungen unternahm. Insgesamt allerdings war auch der Druck sehr groß, daran unbedingt teilnehmen zu müssen, ob man nun wollte oder nicht. Das heißt an allem, auch an dem was nicht interessierte und was man nicht wollte. Und wer nicht dran teilnahm, wurde dann "angezählt", wie es hieß. Man ging bereits in die Schulen hinein, um Kader für die Nationale Volksarmee zu werben, man sagte: Du darfst das Abitur machen, ganz bestimmt, oder darfst in diesen oder jenen Beruf, wenn Du Dich verpflichtest, drei Jahre oder mehr zur Nationalen Volksarmee zu gehen und dort dem sozialistischen Staat treu zu dienen und die sozialistischen Grenzen zu schützen. ■

rigidly streamlined into the pioneers' organization, the Free German Youth or FDJ [Communist Youth Organizations]. The state was very interested in organizing children and youth in this way so that they could be led on the right ideological path. If you look at the SED [Communist Party] party, the FDJ was its recruitment outfit where one could later select party loyalists for the SED. With the pioneers' organization it was similar. In the context of these organizations a lot of things were organized, even study sessions at school, which at times were not such a bad thing. In sum, however, pressure was very high to participate, whether you wanted to or not. That is, in everything, even those things that didn't interest you. And if you didn't join, you were "counted," as it was called. The state even approached children at school age to recruit for the National People's Army, and told the children, "You can most certainly go on in your studies, or you can go into this or that profession, provided you sign up with the National People's Army for three years or more and promise to serve the socialist state faithfully and protect the socialist borders."

WERNER PETERS

INTERVIEWER: If you think about unification today, five years later, has it been more of a positive or a negative experience?

WERNER: Let me say something here. I think

AN ABANDONED EAST GERMAN GUARD TOWER
PRESERVED AS A MEMORIAL IN BERLIN.

> **WE JUST ANNEXED EAST GERMANY TO OUR SYSTEM.**

Germany as a whole, and especially West Germany, squandered a historic opportunity to rejuvenate this country. I mean, something like this doesn't happen to a nation every year or every decade. It mostly happens after some very disastrous event, such as a war and surrender, a revolution, that you may have the chance or the challenge to rebuild your society and your political system. And with unification we had this opportunity. We even had the challenge—the duty—to rebuild or rethink our political system, because our constitution explicitly stated that it was only provisional, and we had to write a new constitution for the unified Germany. What did we do? Business as usual. We just annexed East Germany to our system.

INTERVIEWER: You made the point that for the East Germans it was a revolution, touching every sphere of life. For the West Germans, it has been a tax issue essentially, and the West Germans haven't been touched or felt the impact in the same way.

WERNER: If you ask me whether we in the West experienced the impact of unification, I flatly say no. We did have this kind of experience. There was some kind of enthusiasm during the first couple of weeks and even months, when we were looking forward to something completely new, and there was enthusiasm among the West German population in favor of this new effort, in favor of this new Germany and the people in East Germany. Yet it was the politicians who somehow turned this [enthusiasm] down.

INTERVIEWER: How did journalists in East Germany work? How was a newspaper actually put together?

KADELL: Journalists started their work very early in the day as in any other administrative office. They came in at 9:00 AM, and they left the office at 4:00 or 5:00 PM in the afternoon. This is very unusual, and something a Western journalist would not understand. Then their planning process was different from the one we use. This was done very early in the day at around 10:00 or 11:00 AM, and the paper was put together accordingly. It was a projected, pre-planned process. That means you had telephone calls beforehand, between the senior staff of the paper and the leading party representatives, and the final say always rested with the party. In some instances—I have concrete examples for that—the party official wanted to see an editorial and made changes. So it was not a newspaper man but a party official, working in a different office, who set the tone. It was he who told the paper what to publish and what not to publish.

And that meant the newspaper staff had task sheets. For example, the paper made a plan four weeks in advance to send someone on an assignment, telling him what to do when he got there. He would, for instance, visit an exhibition, talk exactly to this or that person, and was instructed about the goal of the article and the questions he had to ask. The answers didn't matter at all. If the reporter couldn't use the answers, he made them up.

I can give you a funny example, not from Halle, but from the city of Chemnitz. The paper expected a new editor-in-chief from the West. The staffers wanted to be nice. When the editor arrived, he found the front page done for a whole week in advance. You may laugh about it, but to them this was nothing unusual. They had been pre-planning the paper, and they just thought when he arrived that he would be so busy that he wouldn't really have time to take care of all the daily minutiae, so they prepared a complete paper for the whole week.

INTERVIEWER: How do you go about changing that kind of journalistic work ethic, if it's so ingrained and so much part of the culture?

KADELL: First of all, you introduce new wire services with new information. East German journalists had only one wire service, the state-run wire service or ADN. Now they have three or four. So step by step they learn that they can do something else with this information. And, of course, you train them and discuss their mistakes with them, or what is lacking. It just takes time and patience. ∎

PART THREE

ECONOMIC CHALLENGES

SINCE UNIFICATION, GERMANY HAS CON-
FRONTED FORMIDABLE ECONOMIC CHAL-
LENGES. AN AGING POPULATION, DECLINING
BIRTH RATES, AND A SHRINKING WORKFORCE
THREATEN TO HOBBLE ITS ECONOMY. UNIFICA-
TION HAS MEANT INTEGRATING 16 AND A HALF
MILLION NEW CLAIMANTS FROM THE EAST
INTO GERMANY'S GENEROUS WELFARE STATE.

WHILE RECONSTRUCTION OF EASTERN
GERMANY HAS PROCEEDED, A CHANGING
INTERNATIONAL ENVIRONMENT HAS PLACED
ADDITIONAL STRAIN ON THE GERMAN SYS-
TEM. FOREIGN COMPETITION HAS FORCED
GERMAN BUSINESS AND INDUSTRY INTO
PAINFUL RESTRUCTURING.

INTERVIEWER: Man liest ja sehr oft von wirtschaftlichen Problemen in den neuen Bundesländern. Wie sieht es bei Dir und Deiner Familie aus?

CHRISTEL: Das größte wirtschaftliche Problem ist die Arbeitslosigkeit, die zur Zeit bei uns herrscht. Wir sind zum Glück beide nicht von der Arbeitslosigkeit betroffen, aber in unserem Bekanntenkreis sind doch einige davon erfaßt worden und sind teilweise noch arbeitslos. Es ist schon bedrückend zu wissen: Du stehst früh auf, aber Du kannst nicht zur Arbeit gehen. Auf der anderen Seite muß man dagegenhalten: Wir hatten doch einige Tätigkeiten in den verschiedenen Berufsgruppen, die fern jeglicher wirtschaftlicher Basis waren. Die Leute waren beschäftigt, damit sie ihre Arbeit hatten, aber sie waren nicht wirklich beschäftigt. Es war eine uneffektive Arbeit und auf der Basis kann eigentlich kein Betrieb arbeiten, der irgendwo Gewinn erbringen möchte. Infolgedessen und durch die ganze Rationalisierung sowie den Einzug der Technik kam es zur Freisetzung von vielen Arbeitskräften.

Auf der anderen Seite gibt es noch einen großen Nachteil. Viele Betriebe, die wirtschaftlich gut gearbeitet haben und die auch zu DDR-Zeiten noch auf den neuesten Stand der Technik gebracht wurden, konnten nicht weiterarbeiten, da die Eigentumsverhältnisse des Betriebes nicht geklärt waren. Die ursprünglichen Eigentümer waren vor vielen Jahren in die Altbundesländer übergesiedelt oder ins Ausland, und zu DDR-Zeiten gab es keine Möglichkeit, für ihren

CHRISTEL AND GEORGE LÖBNER

INTERVIEWER: A lot is written about economic problems in East Germany these days. What is the situation like for you and your family?

CHRISTEL: The biggest economic problem is unemployment. Luckily, both of us have our jobs, but among our friends and acquaintances, there are some who did lose their jobs and who are in part still unemployed. It is really depressing. You get up early in the morning, but you can't go to work. On the other hand, you have to understand that in East Germany we did have jobs in various sectors which were far from being economically viable. People were employed so they had a job, but they were not really working. Their work was ineffective, and no profitable enterprise can work on such a premise. Due to this fact and because of all the streamlining, as well as through the arrival of new technologies, a lot of the workforce was made superfluous.

There is another great disadvantage. Many firms that did good business and which, even in East German times, had been equipped with state-of-the-art technology could not continue because their property rights situation remained unclear. Their former owners relocated to West Germany or some other place abroad years ago and were never compensated for their property. Since unification many former owners have come back and want to reclaim their land and property. They file injunctions against further operations on their property, or they want to build something else instead there. On the economic side,

Grund und Boden irgendwie entschädigt zu
werden. Jetzt nach der Wende kommen viele
ursprüngliche Eigentümer und möchten ihren
Grund und Boden wiederhaben, und sie verbie-
ten, dort weiter zu produzieren, oder möchten
etwas anderes auf dem Grundstück bauen. Von
der wirtschaftlichen Seite her ist das noch zu
schwerfällig, etwas für die Betriebe zu
unternehmen.

INTERVIEWER: Wie geht es Dir persönlich,
wirtschaftlich gesehen, im Vergleich zu DDR-
Zeiten?

GEORGE: Mir persönlich geht es relativ gut, ich
kann nicht klagen. Wir müssen unser Geld gut
einteilen, um entsprechende Ziele zu erreichen,
wir müssen sparsam leben und können auch
nicht mit vollen Händen Geld ausgeben und
ganz sorglos leben. Wir müssen auch an unsere
Kinder denken, so daß wir für sie eine
Grundlage schaffen. Um beweglich zu sein,
brauchen wir ein Auto, zwei sogar. Meine Frau

all this is still too slow and cumbersome.

INTERVIEWER: How are you doing personally, from an economic point of view, compared to five years ago?

GEORGE: I'm doing relatively well personally. I can't complain. We have to be prudent with money in order to reach certain goals; we have to live frugally. We have to think of our children and lay a foundation for them. We need a car in order to be mobile, even two cars. My wife works in Erfurt, and she has to commute by car every day. I need a car in Ilmenau to take the children to kindergarten or to school and in order to get to work myself. Moreover, we have to pay back a loan. If I think of the supply of daily goods, a lot of things are easier now. This is particularly true for vegetables and tomatoes, which we would never have had during the winter season. What also is new is the constant supply of bananas, oranges, and foreign and tropical fruit in general. Back then, even chocolate or certain kinds of chewing gum—the children would always have liked these things, I remember—simple things like that were not available. Chocolate, for instance, would sometimes cost five to six times as much, if you take just this one example.

NORBERT WALTER

WALTER: I believe it is difficult to get unification really rolling because people thought it would need no effort to achieve it. And this is particularly true for the West Germans. They believed they could just conduct business as usual. The politicians promised that this would be the case, and there was a determination not

arbeitet in Erfurt, und sie muß jeden Tag mit dem Auto pendeln. Ich brauche ein Auto in Ilmenau, um die Kinder in den Kindergarten oder zur Schule zu bringen, und um dann selbst an den Arbeitsplatz zu kommen. Außerdem müssen wir Kreditraten abzahlen. Wenn ich allerdings an den täglichen Bedarf denke, ist doch einiges leichter. Das betrifft zum Beispiel besonders Obst und Tomaten, das hätten wir früher im Winter nie bekommen. Neu ist auch das ständige Angebot an Bananen, Apfelsinen, von ausländischen Früchten und Südfrüchten überhaupt. Selbst Schokolade oder bestimmte Kaugummis—wenn ich an die Kinder denke, wie gern sie das essen—ganz simple Sachen, die waren früher nicht in dem Maße vorhanden. Schokolade war teilweise um ein Fünf-bis Sechsfaches teurer, wenn man das nur als Beispiel nimmt. ■

NORBERT WALTER, SENIOR ECONOMIST, DEUTSCHE BANK

to change the Germans' way of life. And on the other side, East Germans believed that just opening the border would mean you could move to capitalism by taking all the goods and services from the shelf rather than working for them. Everybody had high hopes without being prepared to make sacrifices and to work for it.

INTERVIEWER: What about the assessment of the East? Was the western part of the country surprised about economic conditions, infrastructure, and the like?

WALTER: I guess we were very surprised indeed about what we found in the East, even those who were willing to take a look before the Wall came down. I have friends over there myself. I met with them frequently in the early 80s. In the summer of 1989, I even went on vacation in the eastern part of the country. My own assessment of East Germany was too rosy as well.

INTERVIEWER: How is the unification process going today in 1995? What has been achieved and what must still be done?

WALTER: A lot has been achieved in the five years after unification. The most impressive thing is certainly the improvement of infrastructure. It is readily visible that within such a short period of time practically all the highways of East Germany have been rebuilt. They are up to Western standards by now. So if you are not looking at the parking lots but at the highways and roads, you will hardly notice any old East German cars.

Unification brought about surprisingly rapid changes in the East. Looking at the infrastructure, for instance, their highways used to be bumpy, they were concrete roads, quite narrow and with a lot of curves. Today they are up to

Western standards, they are modern, and you can go as fast in the East as in the West. And something else has changed really fast, even faster than the infrastructure. There was an exchange of the car fleet. Before unification you almost exclusively saw East German cars on the roads over there, such as Trabants. They left a little smoke trail behind because they used really low-grade gasoline. Now you will notice very modern Western cars, not just West German cars but also French ones and many Japanese cars on the roads. It would not be fair to say that all the cars in the East have been exchanged, but if you go on the highways over there, you practically see only Western cars these days.

INTERVIEWER: There has been a great discussion about West Germany's social market economy and welfare state. What is changing? What is staying the same?

WALTER: The West German welfare state practically hasn't changed. Unification was interesting, and I thought it would have been a helpful time to make decisions. For those who studied the German welfare system and its shortcomings before the Wall came down, it was obvious that it could not be sustained. Unfortunately, however, we did not use unification as a possibility to move on to something new and more sustainable. Only now, after we see the budget deficit implications and the necessity to increase tax rates as well as social security contributions to levels that are way above everything in our neighboring countries, do we begin to rethink.

INTERVIEWER: Over the last one or two years, you read a lot about labor costs being a problem for German companies. Many companies have moved parts of their operations abroad.

WALTER: Labor cost is an issue for German firms. It is particularly an issue for those firms which produce goods that are sold or traded internationally. Here, it is very obvious that after unification not only were cost developments in Germany detrimental to its competitiveness, but we also increased our labor costs considerably. We did so in West Germany and even more so in East Germany. Yet this is not the only change that is relevant for competitiveness.

At the same time, the lifting of the Iron Curtain meant that a lot of competitive countries are at our doorstep. We are no longer talking about far away places such as Thailand or Singapore; now they are right at our doorstep. And here, of course, competition is much fiercer, since West German capital could be relocated, for instance, in countries like Hungary or the Czech Republic, which is just an hour's drive away from Germany.

BIRGIT DE LONG

INTERVIEWER: Is German unification a positive thing?

BIRGIT: No, I don't think so. To me the Wall was a way of life. It seemed weird when the Wall fell. It was not my life anymore. Anyway, it went down. When I went to Berlin afterwards I realized what a horrible life they must have had over there.

East Germans that came over to our side, they thought they had the right to get free money from us, get everything they needed, everything they wanted. But it took us 40 years. It took us 40 years to have what we have now. So there is a big—how do you say—bor-

derline between East Germans and West Germans. I think it will always be there. Maybe until the next generation. I will always feel that way. To me, East Germans are East Germans. They're different. They are different.

OTTO GRAF LAMBSDORFF

INTERVIEWER: It seems that in the last five years Germany has been hit by a triple challenge: unification, recession, increased international competition. Why does unification take longer and cost more than many people anticipated?

LAMBSDORFF: First, it is correct that unification is going to be more expensive, more time-consuming, and more difficult. It is more expensive, because we didn't realize how run-down that part of the country had been when the East joined the West. The capital life of the industry has more or less been scrapped. We had to tear it down. And, of course, it takes time to rebuild, but it will have the effect that, in ten years from now, after we have reindustrialized this part of the country, it will be the most modern and competitive among the European industrial sites.

Second, all that is more time-consuming, and we made a mistake, which I think was hardly avoidable. That is, on October 3, 1990, the full West German legal system was transferred to the East. And a run-down country, a rotten economy, such as we found over in the East, with no civil service administration living up to West German standards, could not live with these regulations, with this network of rules and laws and bills and what have you.

It takes time for that. We had to cut regulations and to push them back. I hope one day we will use these experiences to push back regulations in West Germany, too.

German unification proves more difficult because we had underestimated the impact that 40 years of communism had and do have on the minds of the people. Of course, adjusting to a system and to an order of freedom has its advantages, and it is attractive. People can travel, which was one of the major wishes of our East German countrymen. Yet freedom means chances and risks. And risks didn't exist in communist society.

INTERVIEWER: Let me go back to an economic issue in West Germany. You have said that you feel the German economy is overregulated.

LAMBSDORFF: Yes, it is. The German economy is overregulated. We have a huge report from a deregulation commission with numerous proposals to deregulate the economy. The

OTTO GRAF LAMBSDORFF,
FORMER CHAIRMAN, FREE DEMOCRATIC PARTY

telecommunications sector is of course always of interest to American companies as well as the utilities and power plant sector, banking and insurance. We have made progress, but there are lots of other areas where we still have to deregulate.

INTERVIEWER: Let's talk about a specific example. What about shop hours in Germany?

LAMBSDORFF: Americans find it hard to

understand that we have shop hours from 9:00 AM to 6:30 PM, and nobody can buy anything after 6:30 PM. It is a ridiculous situation. But unfortunately it is a symbol of the lack of mobility and flexibility in Germany. The shopkeeper should have a right to say, "I open my shop when I would like to, and I don't need the government to tell me when I have to turn the key in my door."

PHOTO COURTESY OF GERMAN INFORMATION CENTER, NEW YORK

GUIDO PETERS

INTERVIEWER: What is the biggest problem young people have in Germany today?

GUIDO: I think young people in my generation have a lot of problems in Germany, mostly economic problems. It is very hard to find a job here in Germany. It took me almost one year to find a job, and I was lucky to find one. Other friends of mine are still unemployed. Yet I wouldn't blame unification for this. On the contrary, I think it is a great opportunity, and people who are willing to go to East Germany and who move there and live there can find jobs very easily. But most people in West Germany are not prepared to relocate. They want to stay over here. But it is East Germany where the jobs are right now.

ROBERT M. KIMMITT

INTERVIEWER: You talked about 1930s technology in the former East Germany, even though this was the crown jewel of the East Bloc. Can you think of concrete examples?

KIMMITT: To cite an example of this technological backwardness that existed, I recall seeing an elevator operation in former East Berlin that had been purchased by the U.S. company Otis Elevators. Otis had put in a lot of investment, a lot of technology, but there were still parts of that operation which, during the tour I was given, essentially looked like before the unification process. It really looked like you were walking back into an industrial site of the 1930s or 40s or 50s, at least from what I've seen in pictures.

A HOMELESS MAN ON A STREET CORNER IN BERLIN

Another major issue still facing the federal government and the state governments is the environmental degradation that took place in the east of Germany, particularly on former Soviet bases. Most recent estimates are now that there are over $100 billion in clean-up costs that will be required to bring the East up to some form of parity with the West in the environmental area. And, of course, that's an area of considerable concern throughout the Federal Republic. I recall going to a former Soviet base one time and being told not to walk in a particular part of that base. The reason I was given was that gasoline—in this case, jet fuel—at the end of each year, if it was not expended, had actually just been dumped into the ground. Each commander had to report at the end of each year that he had discharged his responsibility, flown his hours, shot his weapons, and utilized his jet fuel.

BURKHARD KOCH

INTERVIEWER: Your life has undergone significant changes since 1989. How were you affected by the collapse of East Germany?
KOCH: I had worked as a school teacher for a brief time, and I returned to the university to do my Ph.D. I finished in 1983. Afterwards, I started working at the Institute for International Politics and Economics in East Berlin, which at that time was the foremost research institution on international politics and global economics in East Germany.

As was usually the case in East Germany, there was almost no opportunity to switch from the institution where you started out. I

really wanted to switch to journalism, and I tried it once, but I didn't succeed because they didn't let me go. I got a clear answer, "If you want to leave the institute, you will not get a job as a journalist, and there will not be an opportunity to return to the institute." It was blackmail.

In the fall of 1989, I was appointed to serve as an adviser to the Department of Foreign Policy and Security Policy under [Lothar] de Maiziére, who was the first and last freely elected prime minister of East Germany. Everybody at that time, I mean almost everybody, not only in East but also in West Germany, thought that East Germany would exist for another five years so that it could adapt to reunification. Together with another friend of mine, I was put in charge of reforming this institute, and I accepted. In retrospect I think it was foolish from the very beginning.

It is impossible to reform a bureaucracy from within, especially in a totalitarian state. It is almost impossible, and that is why I proposed dissolution of the institution. And so, ironically, I worked myself out of a job. I made myself redundant through this dissolution. ■

PART FOUR

UNIFICATION OF THE MINDS

EAST GERMANS HAVE DEMONSTRATED THEIR DESIRE FOR FREEDOM. BUT THE COLLAPSE OF THE FORMER SYSTEM HAS ALSO BEEN A DISORIENTING EXPERIENCE FOR MANY. EAST GERMANS LIVED UNDER THE PREDICTABILITY OF COMMUNISM AND ARE UNFAMILIAR WITH THE CHANGEABLE WAYS OF CAPITALISM.

WEST GERMANS MUST ADJUST, TOO. A CLEAR MAJORITY IN WESTERN GERMANY HAS NO REGRET ABOUT UNIFICATION. OVER HALF, THOUGH, SAY THEY RESENT THE NEW AND HIGHER TAXES LEVIED TO HELP PAY FOR UNIFICATION. THE PSYCHOLOGICAL UNIFICATION OF GERMANY MAY TAKE A GENERATION—OR LONGER.

PHOTO COURTESY OF MARIA WILLIAMS

BRIGITTE: Viele meckern ja nur, weil sie jetzt den Solidaritäts-Zuschlag bezahlen sollen. Die meckern nur darüber, daß sie immer weniger in der Lohntüte haben. Aber selbst wenn ich mal 50 Mark weniger habe, kann ich mir deswegen trotzdem noch vieles leisten. Ich bin zufrieden, oder vielmehr, wir sind zufrieden.

INTERVIEWER: Wer meckert darüber?

STEFAN: Es sind oft die Leute, denen es zu gut geht; die Unzufriedenheit dieser Leute begreife ich nicht.

Die kommen jedes Jahr mit einem neuen Auto an, ob das nun ein Daimler ist oder irgendein neueres Modell. Sie können nur auf ihre Art und Weise meckern, aber das gehört wahrscheinlich zur Mentalität dieser Menschen.

BRIGITTE: Wer hat das einmal gesagt? Die Deutschen meckern und klagen auf hohem Niveau, nicht wahr?

STEFAN: Das hat der Herr Bundeskanzler gesagt, ja richtig. Das hat er sehr klug gesagt. Die Deutschen meckern auf höchstem Niveau. Und da hat er recht, da muß ich dem Herrn Kohl Recht geben.

INTERVIEWER: Habt Ihr hier schon viele Kontakte in Heiningen oder Beziehungen zu anderen Ostdeutschen? Gibt es überhaupt Ostdeutsche hier?

STEFAN: Die Neugier hier war am Anfang groß, als wir ankamen, und da dieser Tennisclub 350 Mitglieder hat, waren die Leute sehr neugierig, zu erfahren, wo wir herkommen. Aber sie waren wirklich nur neugierig, oberflächlich neugierig? Das bedeutet: Es hat sie gar nicht interessiert.

BRIGITTE: Es war zwar kurz mal etwas Neues,

BRIGITTE: Many people just complain because they have to pay the solidarity surcharge [tax] to help with unification. They complain that they have less and less in their paychecks. Yet even if I happen to have 50 Marks [$35] less, I can still afford many things. I am content, or rather, we are content.

INTERVIEWER: Who is complaining?

STEFAN: It is often those people who are too well off. I don't understand the dissatisfaction of these people. Every year they drive up in a new car, a Mercedes or God knows what. They can only complain. It is probably part of their mentality.

BRIGITTE: Who said that once, "Germans complain and lament at the highest standards"?

STEFAN: It was the chancellor who said that, correct. That was a smart thing to say. Germans complain at the highest standards, and he is right. Mr. Kohl is right on that one.

INTERVIEWER: Here in Heiningen, do you have a lot of contacts with other East Germans? Are there any East Germans?

STEFAN: In the beginning, when we arrived, there was a lot of curiosity, and since this tennis club has 350 members, people were very curious to learn where we came from. But they were really only curious in a superficial way. That meant they weren't interested at all.

BRIGITTE: It was something new, briefly, but then they went back to doing business as usual.

INTERVIEWER: And who is to blame for the fact that growing together takes such a long time?

STEFAN: Both East Germans and West Germans, I believe.

aber dann sind sie wieder zur Tagesordnung übergegangen.

INTERVIEWER: Und wer ist Schuld daran, daß das Zusammenwachsen so lange dauert?

STEFAN: Ostdeutsche und Westdeutsche. Beide, glaube ich.

BRIGITTE: Wir merkten das jetzt eigentlich auch an der eigenen Familie, als wir vor sechs Wochen in Erfurt waren: Die Diskrepanzen werden immer größer statt geringer.

STEFAN: Für uns speziell ist es ganz schlimm, weil wir von dort kommen. Wir wohnen hier im Westen gewissermaßen als Gast und fahren wieder zurück und kriegen das Trommelfeuer der Leute aus dem Osten ab, selbst von der eigenen Verwandtschaft. So nach dem Motto: "Ihr seid schon Wessis". Diese dummen Begriffe—Ossi, Wessi! Wir sind weder das eine noch das andere oder wollen es zumindest nicht sein. Deswegen sind wir nach zwei Tagen wieder zurückgefahren. Wir gehören weder hierher noch will ich wieder nach Ostdeutschland.

INTERVIEWER: Wie kommt Ihr zurecht hier in Baden-Württemberg?

BRIGITTE: Ich komme vielleicht etwas besser zurecht als Stefan, denn ich bin schon immer ein wenig anpassungsfähiger gewesen. Sicher sind die Schwaben ein eigenes Völkchen, aber mein Gott, ich komme im Grunde ganz gut mit ihnen zurecht. Gut, viele Bekanntschaften mit Schwaben haben wir eigentlich nicht. Wenn wir privat mit jemandem zusammenkommen, dann sind es meist Leute

BRIGITTE: Now, we can also feel it in our own family, when we went to Erfurt six weeks ago. The discrepancies keep growing.

STEFAN: For us it is particularly bad because we come from over there. We live here in the West as guests, you might say, and when we go back we get criticism from people in the East, even from our own relatives. As if to say, "You are Wessis already." These foolish terms—Ossi, Wessi! We are neither the one nor the other, or at least we don't want to be. Therefore, we left again after two days. We belong neither here nor there.

INTERVIEWER: How are you doing here in Heiningen?

BRIGITTE: I'm making out slightly better than Stefan perhaps, since I have always been a more adaptable person. The Swabians, those who speak the dialect of south western Germany, are an odd sort of folk, to be sure, but, my God, I'm basically getting along with them pretty well. Okay, we don't have many acquaintances among Swabians in principle. When we socialize in private, we meet mostly people from former East Germany, from Dresden or Leipzig. We hardly meet any Swabians.

INTERVIEWER: Stefan, could you imagine you might be better off in another one of the states in Germany, in Hesse for instance?

STEFAN: At first we had been in Hesse, after all, when we spent time in the refugee camp in Giessen. We had an option to remain in that area. It was our fault to move down here.

> THESE FOOLISH TERMS—OSSI, WESSI! WE ARE NEITHER THE ONE NOR THE OTHER

aus der ehemaligen DDR, also aus Dresden oder Leipzig. So direkt mit Schwaben treffen wir uns dagegen kaum.

INTERVIEWER: Stefan, kannst Du Dir vorstellen, es ginge Dir in einem anderen Bundesland besser, zum Beispiel in Hessen?

STEFAN: Wir waren ja zuerst in Hessen, als wir im Lager in Giessen waren. Dort hatten wir auch Möglichkeiten zu bleiben. Aber das war nun unsere Schuld, hierher zu ziehen. Landschaftlich gesehen muß ich sagen, gefällt es uns im Süden Deutschlands gut. Nur die Mentalität der Leute hier, die geht uns schon ein wenig auf die Nerven. Vielleicht hätten wir in Hessen bleiben sollen.

CHRISTEL AND GEORGE LÖBNER

INTERVIEWER: Was bedeutet der Begriff "Buschzulage"; und was habt Ihr zu diesem Thema zu sagen?

CHRISTEL: "Buschzulage" ist eine Bezeichnung, die eigentlich wir im Osten geprägt haben, und zwar für die Beamten, Angestellten oder Arbeiter, die aus den Altbundesländern in die neuen Bundesländer kommen. Es wurde den Leuten, wenn sie hier gearbeitet haben, zuerst einmal ihr normaler Arbeitslohn oder ihr Gehalt in voller Höhe weitergezahlt. Dazu erhielten sie eine Zulage, die sicher in offiziellen Kreisen anders heißt, aber die wir eben als "Buschzulage" bezeichnet haben. Sie bekamen Geld dafür, daß sie in den neuen Bundesländern als Aufbauhelfer tätig sind, um den Fortschritt oder die Technik schneller einzuführen, zusätzlich zum allgemein üblichen Trennungsgeld, das sie ja auch

From the landscape I must say we like it much here in the south of Germany. But the mentality of the people is getting on our nerves. Maybe we should have stayed in Hesse.

CHRISTEL AND GEORGE LÖBNER

INTERVIEWER: What does the term "bush money" mean?

CHRISTEL: "Bush money" is a term we had originally coined in the East. It refers to the civil servants, employees, and workers who come to eastern Germany from western Germany. These people received their full regular pay when they started working over here. In addition, they were paid a bonus which may have a different name in official circles, but which we have called "bush money." They got extra money for helping out in the reconstruction of the East and for introducing new technology more quickly. That was in addition to the relocation money commonly disbursed, which they would also have received in any of the western regions or cities.

GEORGE: This term has a derogatory meaning, since it was supposed to say, "We are going into the bush now. Former East Germany is so underdeveloped. Let's see what we can do over there." Not everybody, but some had that attitude.

INTERVIEWER: How do you feel when you meet a West German?

GEORGE: If I meet a West German, I don't have to see him as a West German necessarily. It is not a matter of having an abstract concept and putting up a defensive wall in the begin-

in einer anderen Region oder einer anderen Stadt in den Altbundesländern bekommen hätten.

GEORGE: Der Begriff ist auch abwertend gemeint, denn damit wollte man sagen: Wir gehen jetzt in den Busch, die ehemalige DDR ist sowieso unterentwickelt, und da wollen wir einmal sehen, was daraus zu machen ist. Nicht von allen Leuten, aber von einigen ist das gekommen, und daher stammt dieser Begriff.

CHRISTEL: Ich finde, wenn neue Technik eingeführt wird, oder es wird jetzt irgendwo ein neuer Betrieb errichtet, ganz gleich ob in den Alt- oder Neubundesländern, kommen immer die entsprechenden Techniker mit, die dort beim Aufbau mithelfen. Dafür bekommen sie auch keine extra Zulage und aufgrund dessen, daß sich in den neuen Bundesländern so viele negative Reaktionen gezeigt haben, in Form lautstarker Äußerungen oder Beschwerden gegenüber der Gewerkschaft, wurde auch die sogenannte Buschzulage wieder gestrichen.

INTERVIEWER: Wie fühlt Ihr Euch, wenn Ihr mit Westdeutschen zusammenkommt?

GEORGE: Wenn ich mit Westdeutschen zusammenkomme, muß ich sie nicht unbedingt als Westdeutsche betrachten. Es kommt nicht darauf an, einen abstrakten Begriff zu haben und erst einmal eine Mauer zu ziehen. Ich finde, das ist genauso ein normaler Deutscher wie jeder andere, und wenn es Probleme gibt, sollte ich mich davon freimachen, ob das mit Menschen hier ist oder dort. Man kann sich unterhalten, kann Kontakt schaffen. Ich finde, wir haben früher genauso gearbeitet wie die im Westen, nur daß die Voraussetzungen unterschiedlich waren. ■

ning. To my mind, he is just as much a regular German as any other. If there is a problem, I have to get over it, whether this concerns people over here or in western Germany. You can have a conversation and build contacts. I feel that back in East Germany we used to work just like they did, only the conditions in East Germany were different.

BIRGIT DE LONG

INTERVIEWER: Can you be concrete. Say a little more about why you think East Germans are different.

BIRGIT: Yes, I can detect an East German by their accent. As soon as I hear somebody speak German, I can tell that they're from East Germany or southern Germany or northern Germany—or where I'm from, here from Frankfurt. We all have different dialects, and soon as I hear that, right away, I find myself being distant. I grew up with the border, knowing there are two different parts of Germany. And to me it's really still that way.

BURKHARD KOCH

INTERVIEWER: You mentioned earlier that a new indigenous East German elite hasn't been created. Didn't East Germany have dissidents, leaders in waiting, like Poland or the Czech Republic?

KOCH: No, not at all. Not to that extent. It's quite easy to explain. It's because we are Germans, and all the Germans who were anti-

communist or against Stalin, even non-Stalinist socialists left East Germany. More than three million people left East Germany between 1949 and 1989, and these were the potential anti-communist indigenous elite.

I think there were many Poles who left their country, or many Czechs who emigrated after the communist *putsch* in the 1940s and in 1968, but these Czechs and Poles were not integrated into their host countries.

People left. They simply left for the West, for the free part of the country, and there were only a few non-Stalinist socialists. They didn't want reunification. They wanted a reformed socialist German state.

INTERVIEWER: Were you a member of the SED [communist] party in East Germany?

KOCH: Yes, I was a member of the Communist Party. That's one fact that is really used as a political tool these days. For instance, nobody asks someone who was, let's say, a Stasi informer what he really did. Did he harm anybody? What exactly did he do? It is enough to say that he was an informer to kick him out of a job.

INTERVIEWER: Would it be more reasonable to differentiate?

KOCH: I mean, the real problem is that the whole debate focuses on the Stasi issue, which is plain wrong. There were many people in this country who were part of the ruling elite. The SED had almost 2.3 million members, and the so-called bloc parties, which were supposedly non-communist, are not included in this figure. So there was an elite of about three million people, and the problem is to ask these people, "What did you do under the Communist regime?" That's one criterion. The second crite-

rion, in my view, is what they did during the revolution, during the time between the fall of 1989 and reunification. This should be the basis for assessing whether someone is acceptable as a civil servant or not.

WERNER HOLZER

INTERVIEWER: German unification took place five years ago. What about the social and psychological problems?

HOLZER: Both of us spoke German, but words had a different meaning in East and West Germany. And people thought it wouldn't be that difficult to overcome. As it soon turned out, it was indeed very difficult. The psychological barrier between the two parts of the country, two-thirds West Germany, one-third East Germany, generated tremendous differences.

To give you an example from my profession as a journalist, magazines and newspapers had expected a new market to emerge, because Easterners were so hungry for information. So, we went in there. And it turned out very quickly that even quality papers from West Germany and TV programs, especially the printed press, had a very hard time selling anything. You know, people were used to a different style, to a very calm kind of government-obedient press, and we in West Germany did it just the opposite way. Easterners couldn't digest it. They didn't even understand that this was democracy—everybody fighting openly, criticizing politicians in a very open manner.

So this was an issue of speaking a different language, a different meaning of words.

INTERVIEWER: Have you or your friends been to East Germany? Have you met people from East Germany?

GUIDO: Yes, I have been there quite a lot. I worked as a campaign aide for the liberal party, the FDP [Free Democratic Party], and actually I was there from the beginning when East Germans had their first free elections.

INTERVIEWER: How are East Germans similar; how are they different?

GUIDO: Since I worked on a campaign in the east, and I also lived in West Berlin and studied there, I had many contacts with East Germans. I also had two East German girlfriends at the time when I lived in West Berlin, but it was difficult for me because the cultural differences were so great. That is to say, Easterners don't have this broad experience. They don't know so many foreign countries and foreign cultures. I've had that experience a lot in my life, and they don't understand when I am talking about America or other

FESTIVITIES IN FRONT OF CHRISTO'S WRAPPED REICHSTAG, MAY 1995.

countries. They don't understand different opinions sometimes, different cultures, and this made living with East Germans very difficult for me, because we couldn't understand each other, and somehow we weren't at the same level.

OTTO GRAF LAMBSDORFF

INTERVIEWER: What about the psychological dimension of German unification? Why is it so hard for East Germans to make the jump?

LAMBSDORFF: Because it is a terrible change for them. People in East Germany have not lived in an environment of freedom since 1933. Only the elderly people, let's say above 60 or 65 years, had the experience of participating in a free election. And to adjust to a democratic system, not just to look to the authorities, is something for which you need a learning process.

INTERVIEWER: Can you say something about the topic of right-wing radicalism and xenophobia in Germany?

LAMBSDORFF: There is xenophobia in Germany generally, not only in East Germany. There is this sense in West Germany, too. I think even the most brutal incidents happened in West Germany. Unfortunately, there is xenophobia everywhere, in all European countries. Yet looking back on our history, I think Germany is the last country which can allow xenophobia to exist and to grow, including anti-Semitism. And therefore we have taken measures against it. In the last elections, right-wing radicals, extremists, and neo-fascist parties did not gain any seats in the parliament.

INTERVIEWER: Let's talk about your city of Frankfurt. Could you name the single biggest problem or challenge concerning the issue of foreigners in Frankfurt?

COHN-BENDIT: I think immigration is always a problem. Thirty percent of Frankfurt's population are migrants so in schools, 40 percent of the students are children of migrants. These are not big problems. They are quite mundane integration problems, you know. I would say Frankfurt itself has no problems. And, at the same time, lots of day-to-day problems. You can solve these problems if you get the policies right.

INTERVIEWER: Some people attribute a lot of this anti-foreigner feeling to the falling of the Wall. Is that subsiding, or is it changing?

COHN-BENDIT: I think five years after unification it is clear that unification brought a

DANIEL COHN-BENDIT, FRANKFURT CITY GOVERNMENT

lot of problems for Germany. It was a good thing, yet it brought a lot of problems. In Germany the danger is that part of the population will make an unrealistic projection. Our problem is not the unification process. It is the migrants. Germany would face these problems with or without unification. I would say that five years after unification we must make a greater effort and explain that this unification project is complicated, but it has nothing to do with migration.

INTERVIEWER: What about the relationship between Germans and foreigners in East and West? Is there more tension in the East?

COHN-BENDIT: The problem is that East Germany was effectively closed for 40 years. It was a closed society. They didn't get used to living with foreigners. Of course, it takes time to get used to living with foreigners. There is less of a problem in a city like Frankfurt than in a city where people have never seen a black or a Turkish person. Slowly, East Germany has to get used to the fact that the closed world, from the days before the Wall came down, has changed.

JULIUS SCHOEPS

INTERVIEWER: Talking about the last five years, what is different in Germany for minorities since 1990?

SCHOEPS: The united Germany is a new Germany now, and in a way it's very problematic for minorities. It's problematic for Jews. Let me talk about Jews here. Until 1989, it was less problematic for a Jew to live in West Germany or East Germany. Both

countries were, in a way, occupied countries with limited or restricted sovereignty. Jews could live here, and they had the feeling that, if there were a problem, the Americans or the Russians were on the scene, and they could help. Yet after 1989, we have a problem. It's a new Germany with full sovereignty, and this is problematic because Jews in this country have to define their position in a new way. What does it mean to be Jewish in this country now? Are they Germans? Are they Jews in Germany?

INTERVIEWER: Let me ask you about yourself. Are you a German who is Jewish? A Jew who lives in Germany?

SCHOEPS: It depends. Sometimes I'm a Jew in Germany. Sometimes I feel like a German of Jewish faith. You will find anti-Semitism in this country, and in some surveys 25 percent of the population are extremely anti-Semitic, and 30 percent are latently anti-Semitic. But, on the other hand, it has changed a lot. I personally made the decision to stay in this country when I came to Germany with my parents after 1945. The idea was to build up a new Germany, and I helped to build it.

INTERVIEWER: Do you personally encounter anti-Semitism in Germany?

SCHOEPS: Sure, it happens sometimes, but it's not a problem.

INTERVIEWER: Do you still have mixed feelings today about a united Germany?

SCHOEPS: At the moment I don't have any mixed feelings because I went to the new states in East Germany. I was one of the first to come here and build up a new university.

My parents and ancestors came from this region here. In a way, I sometimes think it is like a new beginning after 1933. My parents had to leave this country in the 1930s, and to me it feels like coming back.

INTERVIEWER: As a German and a Jew, do you feel proud? Do you feel patriotic?

SCHOEPS: All of it, I think. When I'm proud of this country, I'm proud of German Jewish history, not Hitler. Hitler, that's not my history. My history is that of Jewish democrats in the 19th century and the 20th century, and that's my world.

INTERVIEWER: If you think about tolerance toward minorities and Jews, is there a generational difference in Germany?

SCHOEPS: Sure. There is a problem with tolerance in this country but even among the young generation. Germans have to live with others, to live with foreigners and with other cultural traditions. They have to learn how to do this.

JULIUS SCHOEPS, POTSDAM UNIVERSITY

INTERVIEWER: Germany is experiencing a rising crime rate and violence, not just against foreigners. Is this only a political phenomenon?

KADELL: Violence is increasing in East and West Germany. It is definitely on the increase in the West, and compared to the time before the political change, it is exploding in the East. You have lots of young people who don't have jobs and perspective. The places they used to go have closed down, and new ones haven't opened. There are no independent organizations which they can work with, and that's not good. Violence and crime are a problem.

INTERVIEWER: What about that particular crime that we read so much about in the United States, xenophobic violence and right-wing radicalism? How do you assess that in East and West Germany?

KADELL: Well, you have those things in the East. You have those things in the West. There is no political organization behind it that could really bring such people together. It's a floating part of Germany's youth which has lost direction. For instance, if you ask them about Nazi leaders or their program and what they did, they don't know anything about it. Most of them are not that intelligent and not that well educated, after all. What they realize is that they can provoke by brandishing the SS-insignia or something similar.

It is a selective view that this would be politically inspired crime. The same people who commit these crimes take persons in wheelchairs and throw them down escalators in a subway station. They attack old people. They attack young people, too, and they strike faster

if someone is different. Of course, everybody is complaining now and asking why. Is it the family? Is it the current social situation? Is it the school? What is it, and what can you do? Yet so far I don't see any conclusive answer.

ANGELA STENT

INTERVIEWER: An East German living in West Germany told me, "Five years after unification, I'm still haunted by the experiences I had with the Stasi and with the police state, and I can't go beyond it, and a lot of my friends can't get beyond it." What about the psychological unification, this issue in particular? Does it play a role? Does it mean it will still take a while to integrate the two states?

STENT: I think it will take much longer to integrate the two states psychologically than either economically or politically. Economic integration is taking longer, and it's much more expensive than people thought it would be. I think psychologically it will take a very long time. If you go back, and take the analogy of the post-1945 era, you can say, "Well, Germans had to come to terms with what they did or didn't do during the Nazi era." But then, of course, in the Federal Republic everyone was confronted with that, and they either dealt with it or, in many cases, they didn't.

The difference now is you have this group of 16 million people that not only has to deal, by the way, with that part of their past, which they haven't dealt with either, or their parents' generation hasn't, but also with the whole Communist experience and living in this police state with the largest number of informants per person in the

whole Communist world. I think this will take a very, very long time. And I think that West Germans were not sensitive enough to this at the beginning. I think now they realize what the dimensions are, but they're not sure how to deal with it. And you have an enormous amount of resentment on both sides, East and West Germans, about what all this means.

In my opinion, the psychological wall still exists, and it won't come down for quite a long time. And it may be until the last generation of people who really lived with this as adults and participated in it. Maybe when they're gone, it will. For someone who's 25 now or maybe 20, it shouldn't be a problem. But for most people older than that (and we're talking about quite a long time here), I just think that this is a very difficult and long-term process.

WERNER VON SCHEVEN

INTERVIEWER: When you were put in charge of merging the East German and West German armed forces, what was it like to communicate with your East German colleagues?

VON SCHEVEN: It was a day of mixed emotions, of course, mainly happy emotions. I personally had the impression that the cycle of my life came to a close, you know. I was coming back to the homeland of my younger years when I was a little boy. And I remember that I stressed one point, which needs to be stressed even today. That particular day was the last day we served in the Western Federal Republic of Germany, the last day we served in the old Bundeswehr. The next

day, we would wake up in the new Federal Republic of Germany, and a new Bundeswehr would include the National People's Army [East German Army], and we would have to dissolve their inventory and integrate some of their professional personnel. This was something that needed to be understood. I thought it was self-evident, but later I learned that it was not at all self-evident.

INTERVIEWER: What did you learn about East Germany's defense after unification? What surprised you?

VON SCHEVEN: I think it all boils down to the impression of an intense militarization of the German Democratic Republic [East Germany]. This militarization was so extreme that we had no scale of reference for it. We were educated in just the opposite way.

You know, West German society is not very militarized, and even when the General Inspector of the Bundeswehr, the highest-ranking military official in West Germany, spoke out in public, there were always parliamentarians who warned of a militarization of our society.

INTERVIEWER: How did you rate the quality, competence, and training of East German troops?

VON SCHEVEN: In a professional sense, they had a very high standard. However, I have to qualify that statement. The East German military was subordinate to the Soviet military organization in all operational questions. Their chain of command was the Soviet chain of command, and it ran all the way down from Moscow to the front-line level here in Germany. ■

PART FIVE

A NEW IDENTITY—AT HOME AND ABROAD

OVERNIGHT, GERMANS DISCOVERED THAT THEY LIVE IN A NEW COUNTRY: NEW BORDERS, NEW RESOURCES, NEW EXPECTATIONS FROM PARTNERS AND NEIGHBORS, AND NEW RESPONSIBILITIES. AT HOME, NATIONAL SELF-CONFIDENCE REMAINS LOW. FEWER THAN ONE IN TWO YOUNG PEOPLE IN WESTERN GERMANY SAYS HE OR SHE IS PROUD TO BE A GERMAN. WHILE NEARLY THREE QUARTERS IN EASTERN GERMANY SAY THEY ARE PROUD OF THEIR NATIONAL ORIGIN, EAST GERMANS HAVE VOICED EVEN STRONGER DISSENT ABOUT GERMANY ASSUMING A MORE POWERFUL ROLE IN INTERNATIONAL AFFAIRS. AT HOME AND ABROAD, GERMANY'S GROWING PAINS HAVE BEEN APPARENT.

INTERVIEWER: Besonders in der Presse wird heute manchmal von einer neuen internationalen Rolle Deutschlands in der Welt gesprochen. Was sind Eure Gedanken oder Eure Einstellung dazu?

STEFAN: Ich verstehe die Frage, aber es interessiert mich nicht, wie Deutschland in der Welt dasteht. Ich glaube nicht, daß Deutschland Großmachtbestrebungen hat. Die Deutschen haben so viel Schlimmes angerichtet in diesem Jahrhundert; die sollen mal so bleiben wie sie sind. Wie sie sich jetzt in der UNO oder NATO verhalten, kann ich nicht entscheiden und ich weiß nicht, ob Deutschland mehr internationale Verantwortung übernehmen soll, wie oft gesagt wird. Mag ja sein, daß nicht nur die USA oder Großbritannien und Frankreich Soldaten zu Einsätzen ins Ausland schicken: Ich habe damit nichts zu tun, mir ist das vollkommen gleichgültig. Ich würde meinen Sohn nicht in irgendeinen Krieg schicken, auch nicht in den Irak oder nach Kuwait. Ich würde ihm eher die Finger brechen, bevor er da hingeht.

INTERVIEWER: Maastricht und die Europäische Union, sind das alles positive Entwicklungen?

STEFAN: Ja, ich bin für Europa. Aber ich glaube auch (und da muß ich den Leuten Recht geben, die mehr davon verstehen), daß man neben Dingen wie Flugverkehr oder Reisefreiheit, ebenso den Verbrechern die Tätigkeit erleichtert. Man öffnet dadurch den kriminellen Kreisen Osteuropas, und gerade Polens und Rußlands Tür und Tor, und deshalb sollte man aufpassen. So schön es auch sein mag,

INTERVIEWER: The press in particular is talking about a new international role for Germany in world affairs today. What do you think about that?

STEFAN: The question makes sense, but it doesn't interest me, what Germany's standing in the world should be. I don't believe that Germany has any ambitions to become a world power. Germans have perpetrated so many atrocities in this century that they should remain where they are now. I can't decide how they should behave in the UN and in NATO, and I don't know whether Germany should shoulder additional international responsibility, as they often say. It may be that not only the United States and Great Britain and France should send soldiers on missions abroad. But I won't have anything to do with it. I would not let my son fight in a war, not even in Iraq or in Kuwait, that doesn't interest me at all. I would rather break his fingers than let him go down there.

INTERVIEWER: Maastricht and the European Union, are these positive developments?

STEFAN: Yes, I'm in favor of Europe. But I also believe—and here I have to defer to those who know more about this than I do—that apart from improvements in air traffic and travel, you also make it easier for criminals. The doors are wide open for the criminal circles in eastern Europe, especially from Poland and Russia, and this is why you have to be careful—nice as it may be to drive across national boundaries without having your papers inspected. That was one of the greatest experiences for us when we arrived in West Germany and drove to France after a few days. Nobody checked you anymore, no customs

wenn man über Landesgrenzen fährt und nicht mehr kontrolliert wird. Das war für uns eines der großartigsten Erlebnisse, als wir damals in Westdeutschland ankamen und nach einigen Tagen das erste Mal nach Frankreich fuhren: Kein Mensch kontrollierte uns mehr, kein Zöllner, keine Polizei. Diese ganzen so erniedrigenden Dinge, die ich persönlich erlebt hatte, waren verschwunden. Man wurde durchgewunken, es war ganz toll und ich finde es auch heute noch toll, aber es gibt eben leider Dinge, die aus anderen Ländern eingeführt werden, ob das nun Prostituierte oder Rauschgift sind, gegen die sich der Staat vielleicht mehr schützen sollte. ∎

ANGELA STENT, GEORGETOWN UNIVERSITY

officer or policeman. All these degrading things that I personally experienced under the communist system were gone. They just waved you through. It was a great moment, and it still is a great moment for me today. But there are, alas, things that are imported from other countries, whether it's prostitutes or drugs, against which the state should perhaps be more vigilant.

ANGELA STENT

INTERVIEWER: Five years after unification, 50 years after the end of the Second World War, is there any reason why we should be afraid of Germany?

STENT: I myself believe that democracy and a peaceful attitude toward international relations, if you like, have been internalized. These values have been internalized by most Germans. I do recognize that Germany, in this post-unification era, is still very uncomfortable about what its role in Europe is going to be and what its international role is going to be. And there are things that we don't know that the Germans are still trying to figure out. For instance, what does it mean to be a sovereign nation? Here we are, a large and most prosperous country on the European continent with a lot of unstable countries to our east, with reasonably stable countries to our west, but all of them with certain degrees of economic problems. What is our role? Are we to dominate again? And if so, how are we going to dominate? Because Germany is already dominating the east European countries, economically, though not politically. So what we have to be concerned about is the unknown.

Now, there are some people who believe the younger generation, precisely because it's now 50 years after the war, is not going to grow up with the same political consciousness, with the same feelings of guilt or responsibility. They're going to say, "It's time to be normal. Why can't you just treat us like a normal country?" And we don't know how Germany as a "normal" country, that is to say, without a limit on its sovereignty which it had for 45 years after the war, will behave.

Again, I personally believe that Germans have internalized the democratic values that we wanted them to and that whatever happens in the future, they're not going to go back to some kind of authoritarian or imperial system. But there are others who believe, because you have weak states to the east, you have questions about the military situation of the central and east European countries. You have a very unstable former Soviet Union, such that Germany might be tempted to fill that vacuum. And there are those who believe that the next generation of Germans might say, "Well, why shouldn't we have nuclear weapons? The others, France and Britain, for instance, do. Other major powers do."

Again, I don't think myself that that is a danger. I think the only circumstances under which one would have to be very concerned about Germany in the future would be if there were serious economic problems; I mean a serious depression, inflation. And then these questions of immigration, which clearly now are already an irritant, would become more important. And then you could have someone being elected in Germany who would be much more nationalistic and saber-rattling, if you like. But I think that's highly unlikely.

INTERVIEWER: Some people are fond of saying

the new Germany is not just a bigger version of West Germany. What does that mean?

STENT: I think it means that when unification occurred—East Germany, the German Democratic Republic, was just absorbed by West Germany; the West German political parties took over, and it was thought that it was essentially just a larger West Germany. But, of course, it isn't, because you have 16 million people in the eastern part of Germany who have grown up with a completely different culture, different views on everything, and don't feel themselves part of West German society.

Again, it's generational. It is possible that in 10 or 20 years' time you will have a fully integrated Germany. But I believe that to some extent the views of those 16 million people, even though they're a minority in terms of the larger German state, will have some impact. They may to some extent change, if you like, the political culture of the German state. I don't think we know yet how that's going to work itself out, but it clearly isn't just a larger West Germany.

ROBERT M. KIMMITT

INTERVIEWER: Not everybody was happy about unification in 1990. Margaret Thatcher didn't like it. Mitterrand was very anxious about it. Even German political figures and writers such as Günter Grass opposed it. Was there anything to be afraid of?

KIMMITT: When one looks at the question of German unification in 1990, and particularly the move toward German unification in 1989, from an international angle, I think one important thing to understand is that the United

States had said for 40 years that one of its goals, or one of the alliance's goals, was German unification in freedom and within the alliance. So it should have come as no surprise to people that we were 100 percent supportive of German unification within the alliance. Indeed, George Bush made that statement two weeks before the Wall fell, and that was our guidepost throughout the two-plus-four negotiations, leading right up to the wonderful, momentous events of October 3, 1990.

I think some of our European friends, even some Germans, had differing views about unification. But the fact of the matter is that there was a tidal wave of history moving forward. There was no way of standing against it, because ultimately what unification represented was an expression of the will of the German people on both sides of the inner-German border to be free, to be able to make their own choices. It was a wonderful time to serve in government and be able to support that process.

Perhaps, had we lived closer to Germany and been through some of the difficult times that Germany had been through, there would have been a little bit more understanding for the hesitation. But frankly I'm not sure what that hesitation would have produced, because unification was going to take place. It was only a question of how quickly.

WERNER HOLZER

INTERVIEWER: Germany finds itself in a new international environment today. Could you comment on the current debate inside Germany whether the country should be pursu-

ing a so-called normal foreign policy or not?

HOLZER: To begin with, the question is what is a normal foreign policy? Is it normal to be prepared to go to war? You might argue it is, because the world is as it is. But Germans do have a problem with that, and I think German schizophrenia is haunted by international schizophrenia vis-a-vis Germany. On the one hand, people expected us (and certainly during the Cold War) to be strong enough to stop the Red Army in its conquest of Western Europe. Yet as Willy Brandt put it, we are not allowed to be strong enough to fight Luxembourg. So there is no easy answer.

I personally think Germany has to readjust, not just because of unification. Even before this I had said that we cannot keep hiding in the shadows of our friends in the West, the United States and others, and just keep on telling people that our history forbids us to do the dirty work on this planet.

INTERVIEWER: What does that mean for the question of out-of-area operations?

HOLZER: I think out-of-area operations and the whole set of related issues is probably the most difficult one for Germans, but I do think we have to return to the international fold. It's difficult because I guess you can't blame a country that is trying to learn the lessons from its own history. Our own history in this century alone has really carved deep lines into our hearts and minds. You know, in my country my generation was brought up more in a 19th century-style sense for patriotism and the

ROBERT M. KIMMITT,
FORMER U.S. AMBASSADOR TO GERMANY

WERNER HOLZER, EDITOR-IN-CHIEF (RET.),
FRANKFURTER RUNDSCHAU

CHRISTOPH BERTRAM,
DIPLOMATIC CORRESPONDENT, DIE ZEIT

Fatherland and all of that. During my own youth I started hating these words because they were so much abused. So it's hard for the Germans to readjust, but I think, the world being as it is, we have to return to the international fold even in out-of-area operations.

WERNER PETERS

INTERVIEWER: How do you personally feel about the decision to move the German capital from Bonn to Berlin?

WERNER: I am absolutely in favor of moving the German capital to Berlin, for a lot of reasons, although as a citizen of Cologne and a businessman in Cologne, it will certainly hurt me in some ways. But I think it's part of this preposterous attitude of the old West German political system that they even thought about keeping Bonn as the capital of Germany. Bonn has always been a provisional capital, and it is absolutely ridiculous to say now that we have become so accustomed to it, let's leave it there.

And there is another very important aspect. We have taken away almost everything from the East Germans. We have taken away their constitution. We have taken away their social system. They had a lot of social achievements. We have taken away their pride. We have taken away everything. We even took away some really minor things, which were very useful and very good, because everything had to be just like in West Germany.

INTERVIEWER: Considering the German identity and the loss of German identity, are East Germans more German than West Germans?

WERNER: East Germans have lost their identity in a way, but not voluntarily as the West Germans have. For them, the problem is, of course, more crucial and difficult. They have worked hard, although they may have suffered under the old political system. Yet they took some kind of pride in building up this particular economy and society, and now everything has been declared null and void. So their identity has been completely destroyed.

Of course, our identity was destroyed as well in 1945. And afterward, we learned to live with this kind of destruction, adapting to some kind of new lifestyle and to the new idea of having a political identity as Europeans.

INTERVIEWER: There are some who say that German identity over the last 40 years was an unnatural thing, because Germany was divided and patriotism and nationalism were squelched both internally and externally. There was a big push in many circles for a European identity, a Europeanization.

WERNER: I may be wrong, but I would like to point out that we have not been forced into giving up some kind of German identity or forced into some kind of Europeanization of our identity. This has come naturally over the last couple of decades. What we have now, of course, is some kind of re-emergence of the German identity question. And in my opinion, this is something artificial which is being forced upon us by pundits, historians, politicians, demagogues, and what not. I stick to my point that most people in Germany could not care less about these so-called identity issues, and in a way they feel very comfortable as Europeans and even as Westerners.

INTERVIEWER: Is there a new German nation? A new German identity?

SCHOEPS: I would rather say Germany is on its way to becoming a new nation. It's on its way to a new identity. This will come, I am sure. And I'm sure this new Germany will be part of Europe, of the growing Europe. But what part Germany will play in this Europe remains to be seen. In the economic field, Germany is a very strong power, and it is a problem for other countries in Europe. Yet I hope the future for Germany will be in Europe.

INTERVIEWER: Does the move from Bonn to Berlin symbolize something positive or negative for you personally?

SCHOEPS: Shortly after 1989, I would say I was in favor of a united Germany, but it could also have been two German states. Now we have a united Germany, and it's okay that the capital will be in Berlin, because that's the history of this country. Why not? There was at times the idea that the capital should remain in Bonn. This is one option. Another option would be to move the capital to Frankfurt. This would be the democratic tradition in Germany. Berlin doesn't have such a democratic tradition. It's the Prussian tradition. But we have to show the world that this Germany is not only imperial Germany or the Nazi Germany; this Germany also has a democratic tradition.

There is a difference between the students in East Germany and in the western part of Germany. In the first semester I had to teach here, I had the feeling the young students had identity problems. But that's normal. Their

country had collapsed. They lived in a new country, and they didn't know what kind of country this was. Yet there is a change now. East German students have new experiences. And I think in 10 years from now nothing will be there to remind us of the history of the East German legacies.

There is a growing new scene in this city. This united Berlin is a big city, and in several years' time it will be one of the main cities in Europe, culturally and in the sciences. If you are coming to spend some time in the city and you see the young people, it's nice. I like it.

GUIDO PETERS

INTERVIEWER: When you think about Germany's role in world politics as a young person, do you ever think about German history?

GUIDO: Yes, I'm very interested in history. I'm interested in politics. But I have to say history doesn't play a role in my decisions. I don't think about it. Maybe I like the American way of life. I look to the future, and I don't focus on history.

INTERVIEWER: Do you follow all the changes in Europe, such as Maastricht and the European Union (EU)? Are they good or bad for Germany and for you? Do you feel more German or more European?

GUIDO: That's an interesting point because I think the role of European unification or of the EU has diminished, since Germany in particular is focusing more on German matters than on the European ones. The whole idea of a European community doesn't play

such a big role in Germany anymore. And I think that's really a pity. I personally feel European. I feel very much international. And my friends, too, a lot of my friends feel the same way. This changed completely after reunification. Nobody talks about Europe anymore; everybody talks about the problems we have within our own country, and they're not trying to solve these problems in a European manner.

WERNER VON SCHEVEN

INTERVIEWER: Is it important for U.S. troops to stay in Germany?

VON SCHEVEN: Yes, I think it is important. I have to admit that so far the Europeans haven't put up a lot in times of a crisis. It is one of the historical lessons of this century that unless the United States exerts a certain degree of leadership, the Europeans will fall apart. They will not be able to come to a consensus in really critical situations, just as we are now facing in the Balkans.

INTERVIEWER: In a Europe without American leadership, who fills the vacuum?

VON SCHEVEN: That is indeed the question. I would think that somewhere around the Franco-German cooperation is the place where leadership can be expected and where it has been exercised from time to time.

INTERVIEWER: Five years after German unification, and looking ahead, what would you consider mandatory for German national security?

VON SCHEVEN: The first thing is to maintain the North Atlantic Alliance and the transatlantic partnership. This is no longer

self-evident. NATO is important for our national interests. I think NATO has really been the anchor of stability, and it has the potential to remain the anchor. Therefore, we need to maintain NATO.

ROBERT M. KIMMITT

INTERVIEWER: NATO is one of the common threads between Germany and the United States. Do you agree with the sentiment, "The Cold War is over, NATO should be dismantled."

KIMMITT: I think NATO is as relevant to European security as it was in the past, and if it's relevant to European security, it's relevant to American security. The fact is that when Europeans fight among themselves, Americans eventually get killed, and the formula we came up with after World War II, that is, an alliance of peoples with common values seeking common goals through the use of military, political, and economic means, is something just as appropriate for the Europe of the future as it was for the Europe of the Cold War period and before. And indeed, if we had made that wise set of decisions after World War I, we might not have had the horrible tragedy of World War II.

In the future, NATO clearly must adapt. That's easy to say but harder to delineate exactly. But I think what it means is that again NATO needs to draw on the strength of the common values that it represents. It needs to maintain a central integrated military command, but it must also look at questions ranging from expansion of membership to whether

more emphasis can be given to the political and economic dimensions, even as NATO retains its military uniqueness. That is the task before NATO today. My response to those people who say that NATO has run its course is, Why change a winning formula at a time of continued turbulence and instability in Europe, especially in the east and to the southeast of Europe?

INTERVIEWER: What Henry Kissinger says about the Russians, some people say about Germany; that is, this invitation to normalcy and a greater, wider international role is like putting a drink before a reforming alcoholic. How do you respond to that?

KIMMITT: Those who would criticize Germany's assuming her full panoply of rights and responsibilities as a major nation state obviously do so on historical grounds, particularly in the light of what happened in the first half of the 20th century. What I would say is that there is a fundamental difference between aggressive unilateralism and assertive multilateralism. And what we support for Germany is assertive participation within multilateral institutions toward common goals. That is vastly different from the course of singular aggression that Germany undertook before.

Yet clearly there are going to be areas, for example, where it is not appropriate for German troops to go, because their presence would upset the situation rather than solve the problems at hand.

INTERVIEWER: Is a new German identity being developed through unification?

WERNER: You know, to have a national identity is to have certain symbols or certain enemies. Prior to World War I and even to the Second World War, part of our identity was that we had a common enemy. The French and the British were our enemies.

During the National Socialist dictatorship, our enemy was this kind of American democratic system. We were more in favor of the Fatherland and our ancestors and so forth. All this is now gone. We have really become Europeans. We don't care so much about anything that is typically German. We really feel like European citizens.

Also, we have given up so much of our sovereignty in political terms, and quite willingly at that, you know. Think of the discussion in the United States whether American troops should serve under foreign command; nobody in Germany thinks of this as an issue of similar importance. German troops serve under American, French, Belgian, and British command.

I might be a little bit atypical, but I consider myself a citizen of the world. Sometimes, in a way, I see myself more as an American or a European; but definitely as a European. I wouldn't say I am proud to be a German. Of course, I am a German, and that's fine, but it doesn't make any difference to me. I don't derive any kind of identity from that.

INTERVIEWER: As Germany decides what kind of role it should play in the world, should the past be taken into consideration?

WERNER: No, the past should not play a role. I think times are changing. They are changing so fast these days that we don't even have that much time to look back. And there are so many challenges now facing us that we really have to concentrate on the future and how to come to grips with these challenges.

Of course, we cannot run away from our past and the crimes that have been perpetrated by Germans. We shouldn't run away from that. Yet in terms of looking back and taking clues from how we behaved before, I would think that the past has nothing to offer for us. Nothing.

INTERVIEWER: After unification there was an opinion poll in which nearly two-thirds of all Germans said that the model for their country should be Swiss neutrality. Can Germany play a role like a neutral, provincial Switzerland?

WERNER: I would never think that Switzerland could be a model for Germany. You would have to think of neutrality in military and political terms, and a neutral Germany is almost impossible in the middle of Europe.

Let me dwell on this a little further. I think the Swiss are very lucky and in a way very well-off and very happy. But this neutrality and their never having been involved in anything has led to a certain complacency as well. I wouldn't feel very comfortable with a role where citizens of a nation are led into this kind of complacency and voluntarily give up any kind of involvement in outside problems.

INTERVIEWER: Let's look at the broader issue, German foreign policy five years after unification. Is a normalization occurring, or is there such a thing as a normal German foreign policy?

BERTRAM: Germans who say the country's getting back to normal again are academic writers and editorialists. We are now a normal country and must behave like a normal country. We must behave like France or Britain.

What is normalcy? What does it mean? I think it's a useless concept. It doesn't tell you anything about how a democracy, a wealthy democracy on the threshold of the 21st century, should conduct its foreign policy.

What is the German interest now? Well, that will have to be considered in a different strategic environment, but foreign policy is about interests, was about interests, and will be about interests. If that's normalcy, okay, then we have a normal country, but in that respect, I think we already were a normal country.

INTERVIEWER: Helmut Kohl told me his reaction to people on the Hill who want to bring Americans home and pull out all the troops, "This is a foolish thing and I can only say they ought to be punished for such nonsense." Why is he so anxious—with the Cold War over—that American troops should stay in Germany and Europe?

BERTRAM: Europe is the one place of multilateral entanglement, involvement for Americans. Americans have gone through wars, two hot wars and one cold war in this century, because they realized that what happens in Europe is central to their interests. If

Americans leave Europe, then I think there will be a general retreat in America from the world. It would be costly.

Why do Americans need to be in Europe for Europe's sake? Because you need that balancing effect that America can provide. You need Americans there for the European Union not to be constantly poisoned by the idea that the Germans are too strong and the others perhaps too weak. Such a balance makes differences in power much more acceptable. It's relevant. You have to have America in there because you want to give countries in eastern Europe the sense that their great revolution of 1990-1991, a democratic revolution, of becoming part of the West, is not in jeopardy; and you need America in order to make clear to Russia that her future role as a respected international power depends on civility in Europe. ■

HELMUT KOHL (L) WITH JEFFREY GEDMIN (R)

AN INTERVIEW WITH GERMAN CHANCELLOR

HELMUT KOHL

As Chancellor of Germany since 1982, Helmut Kohl has been a witness to the last chapter of the Cold War, the fall of the Berlin Wall, and the unification of his country. In an interview with Jeffrey Gedmin he shares his views on the five years since unification and on what may lie ahead. The interview was conducted in Bonn on May 31, 1995.

GEDMIN: Herr Bundeskanzler, wann ist Ihnen zuerst klar geworden, daß die Einheit tatsächlich kommt?

KOHL: Daß die Einheit kommt, daran habe ich immer geglaubt, das war für mich immer außer Zweifel gestanden. Wenn Sie mich gefragt hätten, was ich 1988 geglaubt hätte, zu der Zeit als sich schon bedeutende Ereignisse in den damaligen Ostblockstaaten abzeichneten, dann hätte ich vermutlich gesagt, es wird im neuen Jahrhundert sein. Noch in meiner Rede zu den Zehn Punkten im Bundestag Ende November 1989 bin ich davon ausgegangen, dass das in einigen Jahren sein wird, und nicht in einigen Monaten. Als ich damals im Dezember 1989 beim Treffen mit Modrow in Dresden auf der untersten Stufe der Treppe zum Flugzeug stand und die hunderte, tausende, dann zehntausende von Menschen sah, war es mit einem Mal völlig klar: Die DDR ist im Prinzip am Ende. Ich sehe noch die versteinerte Miene Modrows vor mir, als er mit mir vom Flugplatz im Auto nach Dresden fuhr. An dem Tag hat auch er es begriffen, damit war es klar.

GEDMIN: Ist Deutschland heute ein Land?

KOHL: Ja, natürlich. Mit grossen Problemen. Als ich vor vier Jahren sagte: In drei bis fünf Jahren werden wir blühende Landschaften schaffen, bin ich verspottet und velacht worden. Heute bestreitet das niemand mehr. Wobei ja böswillige Leute meine Formulierung immer falsch interpretiert hatten. Wenn der Apfelbaum blüht, trägt er noch nicht Frucht, aber die Blüte ist die Voraussetzung dafür, dass es Äpfel gibt. Jetzt kommen wir, von der Blüteperiode in die Ernteperiode. Weite Teile der früheren DDR

GEDMIN: Chancellor Kohl, at what point did you personally realize that Germany's unification would take place?

KOHL: I had always believed that unification would eventually occur. That was something I never doubted. But if you had asked me in 1988—while Gorbachev was in power and bold developments were taking place in Hungary—I would have told you the unification of Germany will take place in the next century.... In my speech before parliament in November 1989, I was still under the impression that all of this would happen over the course of several years, not several months.... When I stood at the bottom of the ramp to my plane in Dresden, where I arrived in December 1989 for a meeting with [Prime Minister] Modrow, when I saw the hundreds of thousands of people, then it was clear to me: East Germany is finished....I can still see Modrow's stony face, when he and I travelled by limousine together into the city. He also realized what was happening.

GEDMIN: Is Germany one country today?

KOHL: Yes, of course—with big problems. Four years ago, when I said that in three to five years we will create blossoming landscapes in eastern Germany, I was ridiculed. Today, no one objects. My political opponents always deliberately misinterpreted this. When I said blossoming, I meant, an apple tree must blossom before it bears fruit. The blossom must come before the apple. But right now, we are beginning to enter the harvest season. Much of eastern Germany has become one big construction site. You can see development everywhere and this is a good thing. What still remains to be done

sind eine einzige Baustelle, das können Sie überall erkennen, und das ist positiv. Wo wir noch viel zu tun haben, wofür wir viel Zeit und Geduld brauchen, ist das menschliche Miteinander.

GEDMIN: Ein Mann, der aus Erfurt kommt (er ist heute in der Nähe von Stuttgart zu Hause), war Opfer der Staatssicherheit; dieser Mann hat mir neulich gesagt: Ich persönlich kann von dieser Geschichte nicht los. Das bedeutet mir heute immer noch etwas und ich kann es einfach nicht beiseite schieben.

KOHL: Aber das ist ja ganz verständlich. Es ist sein Leben, und er hat nur ein Leben. Das ist eine tief einschneidende Zäsur. Wenn jemand zehn Jahre gedemütigt wurde, wenn er seine Kinder nicht hat studieren lassen können, weil er die Zustimmung der Partei nicht gefunden hat, ist das ähnlich; diese Kinder sind jetzt erwachsen und das Regime ist untergegangen, aber sie haben eben nicht studiert und sie haben nicht die gleichen Berufschancen wie andere etwa im Westen gehabt. Dass da immer wieder Bitterkeit hochkommt, diese Erfahrung ist doch menschlich eigentlich ganz selbstverständlich.

GEDMIN: Wir haben auch relativ viel Zeit mit einer Familie in Ilmenau verbracht. Sie sagte mir neulich: Du musst doch verstehen, das war eine Revolution, keine Wende, sondern eine Revolution. Das hat für uns in erster Linie Freiheit bedeutet, aber es war ja auch eine technologische Revolution. Der Mann—ein Musiklehrer—hat von 1978 bis 1992 gewartet, um sein erstes Telefon zu bekommen.

KOHL: Ja, das ist natürlich für einen Bürger im Westen Deutschlands oder auch in den USA völlig unvorstellbar. In den

and what will require much more time and patience, is bringing East and West Germans together on a more human level.

GEDMIN: We interviewed a family from Erfurt—they had moved to the West in 1987 and are living today near Stuttgart. The husband had been a Stasi victim, having coped with unempoloyment, harassment, and threats of arrest, because of his political views. This man, Stefan, said to me recently, "I personally cannot escape from this history. To me this still means something and I can't just put it aside."

KOHL: But this is totally understandable. This is his life and he only has one life. And this is a trauma that cuts deep....If a man were spied on and informed on for years—I know of many such instances, even within my own circle of friends—if someone were humiliated for years; not allowed to send his children to college, because he didn't have the approval of the party, his children have grown up now and the regime is gone; but they didn't go to college, they didn't have the same job opportunities as others; well, of course he feels bitter. That's quite understandable.

GEDMIN: The family we interviewed in Ilmenau said to me, "You have to understand, this was a revolution, a real revolution for us. It meant freedom, but it was also a technological revolution." This man for instance, a music teacher, waited from 1978 until 1992 for his first telephone.

KOHL: Well, of course, this is completely unbelievable for a citizen in West Germany, or the U.S....On my summer vacation in the Alps I keep meeting Germans who are my age who come up to me and say "hello we're

Sommerferien treffe ich in den Alpen immer wieder Leute in meinem Alter, und dann kommen sie auf mich zu, begrüssen mich und sagen: Wir machen jetzt unsere Hochzeitsreise in die Alpen. Und wenn man sie dann etwas ansieht betrachtet und fragt, 'Hochzeitsreise'? Dann fangen sie an zu lachen und sagen: Ja, wir sind längst Grosseltern, aber wir wollten immer in die Alpen und wir konnten es nicht. Daher holen wir das jetzt nach. Und das kann Ihnen auf der Spanischen Treppe in Rom passieren, am Eiffelturm in Paris, oder am Piccadilly Circus in London, überall. Die Leute waren ja eingesperrt. Und jetzt haben sie den Auslauf in die weite Welt. Das ist eine totale Veränderung der Lebensverhältnisse.

GEDMIN: Wir haben mit einer Frau in Frankfurt am Main gesprochen, einer sehr netten, intelligenten, sympathischen Frau. Sie meinte: Ich habe nichts gegen Ausländer. Trotzdem habe ich ein wenig Angst. Ich habe das Gefühl, es gibt heutzutage zuviele Ausländer in Deutschland, die auf Kosten der Deutschen leben.

KOHL: Ja, das ist mehr als verständlich, weil es ja nicht falsch ist, was diese Frau sagt. Es gibt eine beachtliche Zahl von Leuten, die gar nicht in Not sind, aber dennoch das Sozialsystem ausbeuten. Dieses deutsche Sozialsystem wird sozusagen Hunderttausenden und Millionen Ausländern übergestülpt; es sind viele ehrliche Menschen darunter, genauso ehrlich wie die Deutschen auch, aber es gibt unter diesen Ausländern genau wie unter den Deutschen sogenannte Trittbrettfahrer der Gesellschaft, die nicht arbeiten wollen und das Netz sozialer Sicherheit ausbeuten. In Deutschland können

honeymooning in the Alps." If you look at them incredulously and ask, "Your honeymoon?" They start laughing, "Well, we may have been married decades ago, but we have a lot to catch up on." And this can happen to you on the Spanish Steps in Rome, at the Eiffel Tower in Paris. That may happen to you in Piccadilly Circus in London—everywhere. People were locked up, after all. And now they are free to roam the world. This is a very dramatic change.

GEDMIN: The woman we have spent time with in Frankfurt am Main has told us—a very intelligent, well travelled person—"I must say—I have nothing against foreigners, but I am still a little scared, my feeling is, there are too many these days...too many who live off German taxpayers."

KOHL: Well yes, this is more than understandable there is nothing wrong with what this woman is saying....There are considerable numbers of people who are not needy, but who are exploiting the social welfare state. We are aware of this, and we are busy fixing it. This German welfare system is now being used by hundreds of thousands, even millions, of foreigners—many of them are honest people, just as honest as the Germans themselves—but among these foreigners, just as among Germans, there are freeriders who do not want to work and who exploit the welfare system. And in Germany, they can extract much more from this system than in Italy, in France, or in the U.S. If this woman goes to work each morning, pays her taxes, and sees that there are others who don't work, that is, do not want to work, they don't pay taxes, yet they still receive money

sie mehr aus dem Netz herausholen als in Italien, in Frankreich, oder in Amerika. Und wenn man dann morgens arbeiten geht und Steuern bezahlt und sieht, dass es andere gibt, die nicht arbeiten und nicht arbeiten wollen, aber dennoch Geld aus der Kasse holen, Geld das man ja mit bezahlt hat, dann werden die Leute böse. Aus den bitteren Erfahrungen des Dritten Reiches und der Verfolgung der NS-Zeit haben wir nach dem Krieg bei der Neuformulierung der Verfassung entschieden: Wer aus religiösen, politischen oder rassischen Gründen in seiner Heimat verfolgt wird, der hat das Recht, hier bei uns Asyl zu finden. Und mit diesen Asylsuchenden haben wir hier in der Bevölkerung keine Probleme. Aber es war nie die Rede davon, dass wir aus wirtschaftlichen Gründen Asyl gewähren. Heute sind wir eines der reichsten Länder der Welt geworden, mit einem sehr hohen sozialen Standard. Nun kommen tausende, abertausende und hunderttausende hierher.

GEDMIN: Das Thema Gewalt gegen Ausländer taucht immer wieder auf. Wie würden Sie das Problem in Deutschland mit anderen Ländern vergleichen?

KOHL: Als Deutscher Bundeskanzler und deutscher Bürger habe ich natürlich immer auch sozusagen in meinem Rucksack die Erfahrung des Dritten Reiches. Damit muss man psychologisch sehr vorsichtig umgehen. Aber dass jetzt in Deutschland gegenüber Ausländern mehr Gewalt angewandt wird als in anderen europäischen Ländern, davon kann überhaupt keine Rede sein.

GEDMIN: Patriotismus ist für unsere Begriffe etwas ganz Selbstverständliches. Was bedeutet Patriotismus im heutigen Deutschland?

from the state—of course this would make you angry....After the bitter experience of the Third Reich, we decided after the war that we would always guarantee asylum to those persecuted for political, religious or ethnic and racial reasons. We have no problems with such individuals, who make their way here.

GEDMIN: Now, about the issue of violence against foreigners which keeps coming up—how would you compare the problem in Germany to other countries?

KOHL: As German Chancellor and as a German citizen, I always have the experience of the Third Reich in my knapsack, so to speak. One must be aware of this, one must approach this matter with great care, from a psychological point of view. But to say that in Germany nowadays there are more acts of violence committed against foreigners than in other European countries, this is totally inaccurate.

GEDMIN: Patriotism, it's something self evident for us Americans. What does it mean in Germany today?

KOHL: Well, basically the same it means to you. Except that Americans have a less fractured relationship to their history than we Germans do. Think of the two world wars, the collapse of democracy in the Weimar Republic, and then the Nazi period. And then of course that democracy came into being at the end of World War II under a military government—all this has deep psychological effects. Yet to an average German, patriotism is patriotism just as it is to the average American. In contrast to the American, however, the German finds it harder to deal with the outward emblems of

KOHL: Eigentlich auch das gleiche, was es für Sie bedeutet. Ausser dass die Amerikaner ein ungebrocheneres Verhältnis zu ihrer Geschichte haben. Die Deutschen haben die grossen Zäsuren zweier Weltkriege, zweier Zusammenbrüche sowie das Ende der ersten Demokratie in der Weimarer Republik und die NS-Zeit erlebt. Und dann muss man natürlich berücksichtigen, dass die Demokratie sozusagen unter der Oberhoheit der Militärregierung ins Leben trat. All das hatte tiefe psychologische Wirkungen. Doch für normale Deutsche ist Vaterlandsliebe genauso Vaterlandsliebe wie für den normalen Amerikaner. Im Gegensatz zu den Amerikanern tut man sich bei uns mit den äusseren Emblemen seines Landes schwer. Und das hat etwas zu tun mit der ganzen psychologisch verkorksten Nachkriegssituation zu tun. Damals liefen viele falsche Propheten bei uns durchs Land und predigten schon den Schulkindern: Du brauchst Deine Fahne nicht zu grüssen und Deine Nationalhymne nicht zu kennen.

GEDMIN: Es wird immer häufiger bei uns in Washington diskutiert: Nach dem Kalten Krieg, wozu sollen noch amerikanische Soldaten in Europa oder in Deutschland bleiben?

KOHL: Also, dazu kann ich nur folgendes sagen: Zu den grössten Taten der amerikanischen Geschichte gehört, dass Harry S. Truman und George Marshall den Fehler Wilsons und anderer von 1919 nicht wiederholt haben. Die Art und Weise, wie die Amerikaner nach dem Ersten Weltkrieg aus Europa abzogen und sich in eine isolationistische Ecke begeben haben, hat viel mit den späteren schlimmen

his country. And this has something to do with the whole botched psychological postwar situation. Many misguided Germans were running around telling our children: don't salute your flag. You don't to need know or to sing your national anthem.

GEDMIN: Is it possible to talk about a normalization of German foreign policy these days? Consider Bosnia in that respect?

KOHL: We are on our way to normalization, let me put it that way. And we may have reached the last part of this journey. We have traveled a great distance. Yet history keeps interrupting us.

GEDMIN: In Washington, there is increased discussion about whether we should keep our troops in Europe and in Germany.

KOHL: Well, I can only say: it is one of the greatest achievements in American history that Harry Truman and George Marshall did not repeat the mistake that Woodrow Wilson and others made in 1919. The way in which America withdrew from Europe after World War I and positioned itself in an isolationist corner had much to do with the terrible events that followed. There is no excuse for Hitler, for the Germans, but of course World War II would not have happened if America had shouldered its responsibility as a world power and pressed for stability in Europe. Germans have not forgotten that peace and freedom in the old Federal Republic would not have lasted without U.S. military presence. Without the Americans, Stalin would have marched right through in 1949/50, no question about it. Now we have a new situation: there are people on the Hill—I know there are some—who tell the American peo-

Entwicklungen zu tun. Es gibt keine Entschuldigung für Hitler für die Deutschen, aber natürlich wäre der Zweite Weltkrieg nicht gekommen, wenn die Weltmacht Amerika nach dem Ersten Weltkrieg ihre Funktion wahrgenommen und auf eine mittlere Linie in Europa gedrängt hätte.

Die Deutschen haben auch nicht vergessen, dass Frieden und Freiheit in der alten Bundesrepublik ohne die Präsenz der Amerikaner nicht gewahrt geblieben wären. 1949/50 wäre Stalin ohne die Amerikaner durchmarschiert, das steht ganz ausser Frage. Heute verhält es sich nun so: Wenn es Leute auf Capitol Hill gibt (und ich weiß, daß es solche gibt), die den Leuten in Amerika einreden, man sollte sich aus Europa zurückziehen, kann ich nur sagen, das sind Leute, die wegen Dummheit bestraft werden sollten. Denn Europa ist nicht tot, Europa ist auch nicht alt; Europa steht vor grossen und weitreichenden Veränderungen für eine neue Zukunft. Die Amerikaner müssten verrückt sein, wenn sie in dieser Situation aus Europa abzögen.

GEDMIN: Kann man heute von einer Normalisierung der deutschen Aussenpolitik sprechen? Denken Sie auch dabei an Bosnien.

KOHL: Wir sind auf dem Weg zu einer Normalisierung, so will ich es ausdrücken. Wir sind vielleicht auf dem letzten Stück des Weges angekommen. Wir sind einen weiten Weg gegangen; aber dann holt uns natürlich bereits wieder die Geschichte ein.

GEDMIN: Herr Bundeskanzler, ich bedanke mich für dieses Interview. ∎

ple they should pull out of Europe. I can only say, these are people who should be punished for their stupidity, because Europe is not dead, Europe is not old either. Europe is in the throes of a deep transformation...it would be crazy for the Americans to pull out during this transition.

GEDMIN: Chancellor Kohl, Thank you for this conversation. ■

JEFFREY GEDMIN is research fellow at the American Enterprise Institute in Washington, D.C. He also teaches international affairs and German language at Georgetown University.

A frequent lecturer and commentator on German and European affairs, Mr. Gedmin has done numerous radio and television interviews for stations around the country and abroad. His articles on foreign affairs have appeared in the *Wall Street Journal, Christian Science Monitor, Los Angeles Times, The American Spectator, World Affairs, Times Literary Supplement* (London), *Problems of Communism*, and elsewhere. He is the author of *The Hidden Hand: Gorbachev and the Collapse of East Germany* (1992). He is Executive Editor and Producer of "The Germans: Portrait of a New Nation."